Real Dakota!

ABOUT DAKOTA BY DAKOTANS!

THE LIFE, PEOPLE & HISTORY OF THE DAKOTAS BY THE PEOPLE WHO KNOW AND LOVE IT!

Including the following contributors:

Kevin Locke	Dale Gorder	Audrey Visser
Tim Giago	Leroy Iseminger	Agnes Brewer
Mary Goings	Sarah Gorder	Norma Johnson
Ella Lobben Valnes	Mable E. Knudsen	Violet Valnes Thuringer
Carole J. Holien	Cheryl Evans Hicks	Callie Ann Olson
Kevin R. Kolb	Helen Eikamp	Bernette Rogenes
Helen Lee Johnson	Adeline H. Lamb	Keith Clifford
Gloria Dyc	Gordon Bird	JoAnne Bird
Norma Wilson	Harriet Foss	Helen Svaren
Timothy Rentch	Brent Lick	Geraldine Sanford
Lorna Steckler	Russell Bonander	Berneda Koller
Alan Cvancara	Jennifer Johnson	Erin Jansa
Wendy Jane Larson	Angie Kiefer	Lynne Monfore
Chick Perez	Mary Ann Hofer	Harmony Schuttler
Joshua Johnson	Cece White	

Cover Art by Cheryl Gorder
Book edited and produced by Cheryl Gorder

50 CENTS DONATION WILL BE MADE FOR EACH BOOK SOLD!

Recipients to include:
St. Joseph Development Council, Chamberlain SD
South Dakota Lung Association

REAL DAKOTA!

Published by:

BLUE BIRD PUBLISHING
1713 East Broadway #306
Tempe AZ 85282
(602) 968-4088

Copyright 1988 by Cheryl Gorder
First Printing 1988
Printed in the United States of America

ISBN 0-933025-07-6
$11.95

Cover art by Cheryl Gorder

ABOUT THIS BOOK

In early 1987, Blue Bird Publishing sponsored a writer's contest for Dakotans. The writers whose work appears in this book were selected from the entries in that contest. A special juvenile section in this book shows the best of the entries from kids under the age of 18. There is artwork and photos as well as writing.

Real Dakota! shows more than the fact that Dakotans are a talented group of people. The book shows that we are people who have feelings similar to those of any group of people anywhere in the world—that is, universal emotions. We are compassionate, hard-working, patriotic, sensitive, and fun-loving. And we have our weaknesses, but we are always working towards making things better.

And most of all, the book shows that Dakotans are striving towards better communication between people—bridging the gaps between cultures and ethnic groups.

THE FINAL MESSAGE IS CLEAR—WE ARE ALL FROM THE SAME TRIBE, THE TRIBE OF MAN.

ACKNOWLEDGMENTS

The editor would like to thank her family for support and for supplying art, writing, and photos: Dale Gorder, Sarah Gorder, Shirley Seas, Arlene Seas, Blake Seas, and Gladys Gorder. Many friends also provided materials, including photos: Cheryl and Gary Kettner and her parents, Si and Charlotte Stime; Gordon and JoAnne Bird; Dennis and Lynda Houg.

Thanks to the authors and artists who sent contributions. Each of them possesses special talents and a deep love of their state.

Photo credits are listed beneath each photo, except for contributors' photos of themselves, which were each provided by that person.

INDIVIDUAL ACKNOWLEDGEMENTS

Anderson Benally for the art used with the story "Ten Years Old in Dakota".

Tim Giago for "Time to Enjoy Time", "Indians Just Want to Be Themselves", "Indians and the Mass Media". Each of these selections is copyright 1986 by *Lakota Times*.

The White History Book Committee (White, SD), Fayriene Schafer, director for the photo of Rachel Waldrath and her poem "The Spirit of the Pioneer."

Free Passage magazine for "An Honest Woman".

Memorial Art Center for background material on Harvey Dunn and Oscar Howe. The Memorial Art Center is located on the campus of South Dakota State University in Brookings, South Dakota, and houses some of the greatest art created on the prairie.

South Dakota Magazine for permission to reprint "Spirit of South Dakota" by Cheryl Evans Hicks. This poem originally appeared in the magazine in January 1986.

Agnes Brewer and Mary Goings for their selections from *Womansight:* "God -Lust", "Growth-Time","Lullabye", and "Epilogue".

Audrae Visser for the selections from *Country Cousins:* "Death of an Old Farmer", "To Oscar Howe", "Ballad of Harvey Dunn", "Words to a Little Town That is Dying", and "Change of Form". *Country Cousins* may be obtained by writing to Audrae Visser, 710 Elk Street, Elkton SD 57026.

Norma Nordstrom Johnson for the selections from her 5 volume series entitled *Wagon Wheels* : "My Home Church", "Eddie Just—The Human Machine Gun", "South Dakota Homesteader", & "The Impossible Dream". For copies of *Wagon Wheels,* write to Norma Nordstrom Johnson, Rt 1, Box 62, Eden SD 57232.

The Sinai Historical Committee for use of the "God has blessed America" photo.

TABLE OF CONTENTS

Table of Contents (continued)

SPECIAL JUVENILE SECTION

ABOUT THE EDITOR

Cheryl Gorder's idea for this book came as a result of her awareness of Dakota's growing need for cross-cultural communication. She believes that the more people know about other cultures, the less stereotyping there will be. Instead, there will be true understanding and cooperation. When the myths about other cultures are found to be false, then we all will be more comfortable with people who are a bit different than ourselves.

Cheryl is the author of two other books: *Who's Who in Antiques,* and *Home Schools: An Alternative.* The *Home Schools* book was on the Small Press Bestseller list for two months in 1987. She is currently working on two social issues books and traveling as much as possible.

Spirit of South Dakota
by Cheryl Evans Hicks

This spirit of South Dakota...

It skips over her sparkling lakes,
And runs down her racing rivers.
It whispers among her wavering fields,
And shouts over her spacious prairies.
It croons in her constant winds,
And roars in her raging blizzards.

It shimmers in her starry nights,
And sizzles in her scorching days.
At times it is gentle.
At times it is fierce.
At times it is revered.
At times it is cursed.
But always it persists,
For it was born of a proud land,
And is cherished in the hearts of her people...

This spirit of South Dakota.

This poem originally appeared in the
January 1986 issue of *The South
Dakota Magazine* and is used with
their permission.

Cheryl Evans Hicks, after 20 years of wandering through New Mexico, California, Hawaii, and Germany, recently returned to her native Yankton with her young son to replant her roots. She is currently a graduate student at USD and has had writing published in several magazines, including this poem .

SMALL-TOWN GROCERY
By Kevin R. Kolb

Shopping time.
Lowly little old gray bugs are flushed from hiding—
years are concentrated on getting about.
His ears are permanently bent down
from centuries or wearing
seedcorn caps as far down as they will go.
Her scarf is like a gauzy cobweb.
Big, black purses clutched tight.
To Shoe's Grocery!
Pink and chrome and tailfins
wheezes out of yesterday.
Noisy little Ford
ever-so-slowly labors down the street.
"Guten Tag! How about dat veather?"
Kuchen and eggs and onions and black coffee.
Cows, weather, that '48 crop
sprinkled in their eyes
and about their silver hair.
They walk slowly and smile for a brief moment.
Another week's groceries
and they go into hiding again.

Kevin R. Kolb has a head-start on his chosen profession of writing. At 18 he is already a published poet and a part-time columnist for a local weekly newspaper. This Leola, SD youth plans to major in English in college.

IT'S HARD TO KISS A FARMER

Helen Lee Johnson

Helen Lee Johnson knows well the meaning of being a farmer's wife. She is married to long-time Estelline, SD farmer, Arnold Johnson. Helen's other interests include being a member of the popular SD Old Time Fiddlers, for which she sings. A song about the group that she wrote is now used as its theme song at the state contest each fall in Yankton. Helen also contributes her time to helping promote tourism for the state.

Whiskers on his weathered chin
    and underneath his nose,
which makes it pretty risky
    for a wife to come too close!

Grease upon his denim jeans;
    just covering his hands—
he's had to fix the mower
    and it's slowing up his plans.

It's hard to kiss a farmer
    when you're dressed to go to town,
an arm around her shoulder
    could cause a wife to frown.

And then the week is over
    Hubby's all dressed up for church,
you can't believe his neatness
    as for field dirt you search.

He looks so clean and handsome
    you're proud of him, it's plain,
And it's great to kiss a farmer
    when the dirt's gone down the drain!

FLICKERTAIL STATE

Harriet Foss

The land where herds of buffalo
    Thundered 'cross the plains,
The land where Indians braves
    Hunt wild life for their gains.

The land where settlers came to dwell
    To break and till the sod,
The land where hearts are laden
    With thankfulness to God.

The land that Teddy Roosevelt
    Was proud to call his home,
The land of countless famous folks
    Who never cared to roam.

The land of the Peace Garden
    Of doves and flickertails,
The land of dew-kissed roses
    Along the prairie trails.

The land of warbling meadowlarks
    O'er waves of golden grain,
The land of graceful white-tailed deer
    Of rainbows after rain.

The land of parks and colleges
    Of Garrison and oil,
The land of opportunity,
    Devotion, love and toil.

The land of fleecy, frothy clouds
    Drifting 'cross the sky,
Or the silence after stormy days
    To thrill the searching eye.

These grand wide open spaces
    Of prairie, badlands, trees,
With birds and creature species
    And the unpolluted breeze.

We love our North Dakota
    So refreshing to endure,
The changes of the seasons,
    Each has attributes so pure.

There are challenges for everyone
    While working or at play,
But we're content to meet them all
    Eagerly each day.

"Liberty and union
    Now and forever more
One and inseparable"
    Our motto, as of yore.

Thank you, North Dakota
    For being what you are,
You're the favorite of all of us
    Of the fifty you're the star!

We extend congratulations
    Now that your birthday's here,
One hundred years since statehood
    In our USA so dear.

NORTH DAKOTA by Harriet Foss

Harriet Foss has not only had poetry and articles published in English, but also in Norwegian. Some of her projects have included editing a county history book and a city centennial book. She is a genuine native North Dakotan.

North Dakota's summer
how breathtaking to see,
With rains or perfect sunshine
and winged things flying free.
The awe-inspiring sunsets with
transparent, brilliant hues
Or the flawless blended rainbow
across the sky of blues.

North Dakota's autumn
what splendor to behold!
With nature's panorama
of browns and reds and gold.
The harvest is upon us
with bounty for each month,
The trees will soon be naked,
the birds migrating south.

North Dakota's winter
the snow, the ice, the cold,
Where arctic sports provide such fun
for the youth and for the old.
The landscape can be peaceful,
restful and serene,
Or changed by raging snowstorms
to jeopardize the scene.

North Dakota's springtime
makes all things come to life,
The prairie lifts her soul to give
to us the fruits of strife.
Again the sweet wild flowers
all stand in bright array,
All slumbering life quickens
at dawning of each day.

Bounteous North Dakota
complete with climate change,
A locality with various scenes
woodlands to open range.
What pleasure and contentment
can come to those who dwell here,
We work, we play,we sing, we pray
and exclaim, "We like it well here!"

Photo: Cheryl Gorder
The Missouri River has been the "best kept secret" of
the Dakotas.

Callie Ann Olson is a confirmed "river rat". She and her family can be found fishing, skiing, and swimming in the mighty Missouri whenever her husband can take a break from farming. Callie says about the river," Living on the river is one of South Dakota's best kept secrets. I can't imagine living without its beauty."

TEN YEARS MARRIED
Callie Ann Olson

a warm summer evening
we hang our legs
over the side of the dock
you labored so hard
to create
we feel the cool water
of the Missouri
rush past our skin

you have taught me to love
this eccentric river
you have grown up loving it
you know its curves
and textures
patterns and nuances
as well as you know
my own

and in this sunset hour
the quiet and swift
current of your love
rushes past me
unspoken
the labor of our lives
together

CRAZY HORSE
Helen Eikamp

His promise of a dream still waits
on Thunderhead, high mountain
in the Black Hills of Dakota.
Its silent, patient vigil keeps,
waiting...waiting...for the dreamer sleeps
enslaved no longer to the tons
and tons of stubborn, granite rock,
loud blasting and chipped carving,
sharp chisel and ear-piercing drill...
and a faith that sweat to move a mountain.

A vestige of that promise still stands
enshrining Crazy Horse (Great Sioux)
in the Black Hills of Dakota.
Korzak Ziolkowski's noble vow,
too grand for one man's time, it now
awaits another sinewed arm and soul
to conquer Thunder Mountain
and carve the white man's monument
to valor and the honored name
of that fearless, proud Dakota Sioux...

Helen Eikamp is a Britton, SD writer who is very productive. She has had poems published in *Pasque Petals, Submit, Inkling Anthology, The Christian Writer, Prairies Magazine,* and more. She is also the author of three books: *The Church Year in Scripture, VErse, Showers 'n Anniversaries 'n Things, Program Bits 'n Pieces.* She is currently working on a book about South Dakota.

Crazy Horse

TEN YEARS OLD IN DAKOTA
Dale Gorder

Little ripples traveling in round circles; ker-plunk! Another rock went into the pond, sending even larger ripples out in the shape of a larger circle that over-ran and swallowed the first one. A small water bug struggled for survival in the long stems of grass near the side of the creek. Ker-plunk! There! One less of those ugly little things messin' up the water now.

Walking on the bank of the creek, you could see the bottom.Once in a while a frog would jump and you'd see him hit the water and disappear in the cloudy water. Sometimes they'd sit on the bottom and look up at you, and wait for you to pass on before returning to the edge to lay in the sun. Other times they'd make a circle and you could see the water fishtail as they'd swim under-surface for another spot on the bank.

Dale Gorder, although he has traveled extensively, draws on his Dakota childhood for his writing.

They were always hard to catch. You had to come across one that was asleep in the sun and if you were real quiet you could sneak up and lunge with cupped hands. Sometimes you'd have one, other times- -splash, and they're gone!

If you caught one though, you could plan the next couple of hours decidin' what to do with him. If he that sorry look on his face or got hurt a little in the capture, you let him go, especially if the air was moving. Something about the air.

If the frog was bright green you took him home. Yup, straight across the pasture up to the yard to find a can. Coffee cans worked the best, if she had one.

Grasshoppers flying around jumping from grass to grass all different sizes. Some of them look like helicopters. Hope I never get one of those big ones down my shirt. I don't wear 'em when I'm pasture walkin' in the summer, but my pants get to hangin' kinda low and I'd sure hate to have him buzz down the back of 'em. Gotta remember to keep 'em pulled up.

What I'd really like to find is a turtle. I know there's one down at the bridge pond, but there's a rock in the middle and he's always out there sunning himself. I guess he's just too smart to sleep on the edge of the pond where I might sneak up on him.

I wouldn't hurt him, though. I'd just take him home and build a pen and play with him and look at his green color. When you turn him over he'll have a splash of orange on his undershell. Too bad he doesn't have one on the top of his shell too, but I guess green is nice.

The air is moving nice now. The grass is bending lightly and you can hear the meadowlarks talking. It must be that they're talking. But why do they always say the same thing? Twee-to-tee, tweetle-te-do! Listen to that. It almost sounds like they're asking a question. I wonder if I learn how to say it like they do if I'll find out.

Practice, practice, practice, and half an hour later I think I have it down pat. Twee-to-tee, tweetle-te-do! Heck, if you were standin' off and didn't see me, you'd swear you were hearin' a meadowlark. I know they think I did well because they answered back. Even the meadowlarks turned and smiled. There seems to be one every fifty feet or so on the pasture fence. The gophers seem to think they're a big pain because their whistles just seem to get drowned out.

I know, I know. I'm looking. OK, OK. I see him, not more than three feet ahead of me on the edge of the creek, sleeping on the mud. Now, quiet! Don't say anything more. Don't even breath! Please, steady my hands and don't step on anything crunchy. That means you too! Now promise not to warn him again! OK, yi, got him!

It's all I can do to get my hands around him. He's the biggest one I've ever seen, and he's bright lime green. Look at those legs, they must be eight inches long. Look at his feet, he looks just like he has a pair of swim fins on. OK. Now if I can get him back across the pasture to the house. Boy, I hope Mom's got a can.

Wait'll Dad sees this. Is he ever gonna be proud!

Yeah, I know. I'll be careful with him. It's OK. I'll get a nice can with a little water in the bottom and a little gravel and a lid and I'll keep him nice for a while and then I'll bring him back. I promise, I promise! Look, I learned to do it like the meadowlarks, didn't I? OK, I'll practice while I'm walking, just listen. But don't make him jump out of my hands. Now if I can just get through this barbed-wire fence without dropping him. OK, you will? OK, I'll crawl through and you kinda talk to him and calm him. Yeah, thanks, just a little ways farther now.

"Mom! Mom! Have you got a coffee can? Mom! Mom! Have you got a can?"

"What's the matter? What are you yelling about? I was in the bathroom and I heard you yelling."

"Well, I caught him and I need a coffee can. Isn't he a good one? Look at him, how big he is. Look at what color he is. I've never seen a frog so nice. Have you, Mom? Have you got a can? A nice big one with a lid?"

"Well, I've got a small one that I just emptied with a lid."

"But I need a large one, Mom. I promised I'd put him in a large one."

"Who'd you promise?"

"No one, I mean nobody?"

"WHO'D YOU PROMISE?"

"NO ONE, I MEAN NOBODY."

"Were you down there with your cousins? I told you, you could go to the creek by yourself. I didn't say to walk way over and get your cousins and then go to the pasture! I'm not going to let you go down there again if you can't listen to me and take orders!"

"I...but I wasn't with my cousins. I was by myself. I just need a large coffee can."

"This is what I have. It's a small can. Put him in here and he'll be fine."

"Well, I..."

"Be careful because the ring is off and it's sharp on the edge of the can when the lid is off."

"OK."

I put a little water in the bottom and some gravel and set him in there. I felt kinda bad though because he didn't have much room in there. I put the lid on and then poked a few air holes so he could breathe. I just set him on the floor in the garage by the wall.

I looked towards the pasture and I could see 'em out there looking towards the house. They never got any closer than that. They seem to like staying out in the open. They weren't happy and they didn't seem sad. They were right and they knew it. The air was moving and their black hair was shimmering and waving just like the bright green prairie grass. Then they were gone and the grass quit moving and the breeze died.

I went to find Dad. I looked all around the farm buildings but I couldn't find him. I called, "Dad, Dad, Dad!" As I called the breeze came up again and helped to carry my voice, but he didn't answer, so I went to the house and asked Mom where he was. She said he was gone but he'd be back late tonight.

I walked to the edge of th pasture and looked out and the breeze told me it would be OK and that he was alright. Well, it didn't really, but I knew he was OK. So I went into the house for the night.

Darkness fell around our house and they moved up around our house. There were no curtains on our windows and it was black outside. Sitting in the house you could see a window no matter which way you looked. They could see in, and we could see out, and I could see them. They made me feel good.

*THEY COULD SEE IN, AND WE
COULD SEE OUT, AND I COULD
SEE THEM. THEY MADE ME
FEEL GOOD.*

Once a man who lived in a city came to visit at night and he seemed kinda skitterish, sitting there looking at a black window with no curtain or shade. He said his wife put curtains and shades on all over the windows first thing when they moved in, never know who's lookin' in. My mother and father just looked at him and said that way we can see if someone drives in the yard at night because we'd see their lights. The guy said wouldn't you hear the dog bark? Dad said, yeah, but we like to see out.

Everyone just kinda looked at each other. Mom and Dad knew about them. They had to. They were here long before I was. They never mentioned them. Nobody did. But the people who lived in the country didn't have to talk about everything. It was enough to know.

We went to bed and later on Dad came home sometime in the night. I had my windows open in my bedroom, one on each side of my bed. There was a breeze blowing through my room and it felt good. They told me when he was home and I smiled in my sleep.

Morning came and Dad announced we were going to the lake. I kinda hated to go in some ways, but if I went I could swim, and being the youngest I didn't have any choice anyway, so off we went. In and out of the water all day, I grew very tired. I didn't like to get that tired because I hadn't been to the pasture yet that day and there were things I needed to do. I missed my big green frog and I hadn't gotten to show it off to Dad yet. We drove home and parked the car in the garage. We carried picnic containers into the house and as soon as we had them in, I said, "Dad, I want to show you something."

I went to the garage to get my frog. As I stepped out into the air, I noticed the wind was really blowing, but I was tired and I didn't listen. Coming around the corner of the car, I looked down at the coffee can on the floor by the wall. The lid was off and the can was empty except for water and gravel.

I walked past the can. He must have jumped in the can and knocked the lid off and then jumped out. The coolness of the garage floor cement felt good on my bare feet after a hot day at the lake.

Walking backwards and looking, thinking he must be here. I know he's here. I have to show him to Dad. He hasn't seen him. He'll be proud of me. Where is he? And the wind blew. Dust was in my eyes from the garage. I stepped backward on a rollerskate my brother had placed there. My left foot was flying out from under me but my right foot was coming down behind me, trying to find something solid to keep me from falling.

I felt pain in the middle of my right foot. I looked down and saw I was standing on my right foot on top of the coffee can. The razor-sharp edge had sliced deeply into my bare foot. The wind had stopped; it became very quiet. I could feel my leg getting warmer. As I looked down into the can the frog water had turned into a crimson pool. I was afraid. They weren't talking to me and I was so tired. I reached down and pulled the can off my foot and the blood poured out onto the floor.

I felt bad. I didn't like to leave water running in the faucet because it wastes it; water is so clean. Now my blood was running and I had no way to turn it off. Now I would never be able to show my Dad the frog. He wouldn't be proud of me for letting him escape, and he wouldn't be proud of me for letting my blood run.

Look! Now it's getting all over the garage floor. I'm tired and they're not even talking to me. I'm sad and I feel like crying. My leg is getting hotter. I better go outside on the grass because I'm getting blood all over and I don't want to make any more mistakes because I've already done so many things wrong.

I limped around the corner of the garage out onto the grass and I could see the pasture. The breeze started to come up and it made my hot throbbing foot and leg feel a little cooler. I stood on one leg with the other bent at the knee. Blood was running off my foot and it tickled like little fingers.

I looked down and I could see her kneeling beside me with her hands on my bloody foot. She smiled at me. Her long black hair was almost to her waist. She was the same age as me and when she stood she was the same height. It made me feel better to be with someone who understood.

She knew pain and happiness and frogs and creeks and ponds and blood. She smiled again and took my hand and pointed to the pasture. I saw them all now. They were everywhere. We walked towards the pasture. My leg felt cool now. The wind was blowing. As I looked down I could still see the blood running from my foot. It landed on the green grass and left a trail. I smiled and thought, that's good because I can always find my way back, if I want to go back.

We crossed the fence and walked a ways into the pasture. She sat down and I sat beside her. She was still smiling. I could see their faces clearly now. Some were happy, some were sad, some showed no sign of emotion. But they all cared, and they were all right. My foot feels good now. I feel only the sadness left from the pain and there is a scar.

Now I understand why the meadowlarks ask questions and why the turtles sit in the middle of the pond on a rock. They miss the people of the plains. And when the wind blows you can hear us, and if you look out a dark window at night when the breeze is blowing, we'll be watching.

Photo: Cheryl Gorder
This painting by Anderson Benally shows the spiritual side of Dakota life. Benally is a Navajo artist now living in South Dakota.

Photo: Cheryl Gorder

Painting inspired by the Black Hills by artist Randy Poirier.

A VOTE TO RELOCATE THE U.S. CAPITAL TO SOUTH DAKOTA
Helen Svaren

I would like the Congressmen to consider moving the capital of the United States to South Dakota. I'm surprised no one thought of the obvious advantages before. My brain is not orginarilly fertile soil for brainstorming, but this time I have hit the jackpot. Before you disagree with me, please listen to my reasons.

Capitals are usually located near the center of each nation. If not, they should be. South Dakota is geographically the center of the United States. This move would then evenly distribute costs of tranportation for the majority of our Congressment. More of our governmental workers would then be closer to their offices. Believe it or not, we've had cars long enough to know how they operate. Two interstate highways transect our state. Citizens who make the trek to the capital to voice their opinions on important issues would have less distance to travel. Think how easy it would be for these concerned people to make themselves heard and thus further the democratic process.

Many credit card operations have headquarters in this state. Since our federal government traditionally operates in the red, it would inevitably be easier to obtain financing. We are obligated to try every method possible to balance the national budget.

Just think, those big industrialists in the East and the West would learn where South Dakota is. From my experience, many people living in the extremities of the United States think that there is only one large territory, called Dakota. They have ignored us so long that, in their thinking, we have ceased to exist. We who live here now experience an identity crisis. Twins are not a single entity and South Dakota is NOT the same as North Dakota, just as California is not New York.

I can assure you we are patriotic citizens. Where else could you find a granite mountain with four presidents carved on it? Certainly this qualifies us for patriotism. If not this, what would? It's time for South Dakota to get some positive national attention. Calvin Coolidge spent vacation time at his summer White House in the Black Hills. Since then, no president has given South Dakota more than a passing remark.

If the capital were in South Dakota, it would be farther from the Soviet Union. It would then be more difficult to them to bug our governmental offices. It would take longer to even find South Dakota.

According to the latest report on ACT scores for high school graduates, South Dakota ranks fifth. I tell you this because some may think that South Dakota is populated only by ignorant cows. Obviously, that is an erroneous assumption. We are intelligent, alert, and hard-working. In spite of this, we would make ideal governmental employees.

The average income per family in South Dakota is near the lowest in the nation. This move would, therefore, save our federal government many dollars. They could save much money by hiring South Dakotans for go-fers. I already told you that we are not a rich state, but I hasten to add, we have the largest gold mine in the Western Hemisphere.

Real estate is inexpensive in South Dakota. Parking lots could abound. Think how economical it would be to acquire sufficient space for a well-planned capital layout. All they would need to do is to move a few cows. I admit that there is a place in South Dakota called the Badlands, but those of us who have visited there agree that even that area is not really bad.

South Dakota does not excel in size or population. I must tell you, however, that we do make the *Guiness Book of World Records* in a few things. We are first in the production of oats, rye, and geese. We rank second in our huge harvest of flexseed and third in honey and sunflowers. From this, you will conclude that we have sufficient moisture to produce excellent crops.

We have unlimited opportunities for hunting and fishing. National sportswriters even call South Dakota the pheasant capital of America. Out-of-state hunters come in droves to match wits with our wily ring-necked roosters. Yes, we have also heard of Jane Fonda's workout, and we have aerobic classes. We might need to construct some tennis courts, but there is plenty of room for several large golf courses. No tee off time would be wasted. The Congressmen would not have to miss votes on important issues when they have the urge to feel the wind under their wings.

The four dams along the Missouri River supply us with an abundance of pure water and economical electricity. The four Great Lakes, created by those dams, total over nine hundred square miles of surface water and 2,300 miles of shore line. Not a person since Noah has seen so much clear, clean water.

The Sunshine State is our nickname. With sunshine about 62% of the time between sunrise and sunset, our air is usually clear with excellent visibility. We are free from pollution, typhoons, hurricanes, and crime. Can any other state match these credentials? Although I hasten to admit to an occasional tornado and a few blizzards.

I hear you saying that the cost of moving would be exhorbitant. I have the answer to that too. Capital buildings are usually dome buildings. The University of South Dakota, located at Vermillion (yes, we have several institutions of higher learning) has a dome building. If a dome is insisted upon, this is an excellent solution to the expense problem. With all of the money that is saved, more revenue would be available and, who knows, they might even lower our income taxes.

Even the name Dakota has recently taken on new connotations. When the Dodge marketing experts searched for a name for their new Dodge pickups, they chose Dakota. To them that name is synonymous with sturdiness and dependable performance. An elite St. Paul restaurant has also recently been named Dakota. The ring of the word Dakota, which is an Indian word meaning friend, has become trendy. In our time Dakota does not mean that only the heads of coyotes break the horizon. We are finally gaining some well-earned recognition. It's about time.

I plead with all South Dakotans to rally behind this super idea. We must make the other forty-nine states aware of what we have to offer. They will then agree that in the universe, we are the center. On second thought, they may even learn that there is actually a **SOUTH DAKOTA!**

Helen Svaren has lived in South Dakota since 1951 and is married to a Lutheran pastor. She has written for the Dakota History Conference and has been published in the *South Dakota Magazine, Good Old Days,* and *Plainswoman.* Her obvious sense of humor is apparent in this whimsical essay.

South Dakota State University's Coughlin Campanile in Brookings is a state landmark. The new Alumni tower is on the right.

Photo: Cheryl Gorder

The University's famous annual homecoming, Hobo Day, brings out creativity in its students. Here the 1986 Hobo Day King and Queen, Blake Seas and Kari Christenson, show their stuff.

Photo: Arlene Seas

"Our Church by the Side of the Road" is dedicated to Sterling Church, located 10 miles north of Brookings, SD on old Highway 77. Keith Clifford, author of this poem, still attends this church. The church has seen many families through good times and bad, as the poem will tell. Keith tells about the evergreens that stand on the north side of the church. They were planted 40 years ago by his Dad and his Uncle. As Keith water and hoed around them as a youngster, he often wondered if they would survive. He reports that "they have just as the church has".

Keith Clifford and his wife Marilyn have raised five children and are now raising their granddaughter, Amy. They farmed until 1981 when poor prices forced them out. Keith started trucking and has trucked through all 48 continental states and Canada, but, "It's always heartwarming to come home." Keith shares with us some very personal poetry, including three pieces we call the "Family Trilogy". By the time you finish reading his poetry, you'll feel like you know this warm man very well.

OUR CHURCH BY THE SIDE OF THE ROAD

Keith Clifford

A Church was started in years gone by
Only a dream in someone's eye
But with hopes and prayers and many a sign
It finally took form under the Dakota sky
Just a small building beside the way
Where oldtimers came, their cares to lay
My folks loved this church and served with the best
And when their lives were over, it gave eternal rest
I was taught to love her simple ways
All through my youth and early married days
It served our needs and buried our Son
Where he joined so many other precious ones
But I drifted away as I grew older
Thought I could make it without the Almighty shoulder
I guess I thought she didn't care
Just didn't have anything more to share
But after forty years I started to see
Many of the things she had done for me
Even if older the friends were still there
Waiting and willing their love to share
The Church still stands by the side of the trail
Her evergreens also, they've withstood the gale
So many sad times have been within her walls
But happy ones too, that have touched us all
I've come home from trucking, all tired and spent
Even though things I've seen happiness rent
I go by the church and imagine I see
A faint light shining just for me
On just a little way down the path
I find my home and rest at last
So ever on this trip of life
That takes us both to joy and strife
We should remember that we have two homes
The one here on earth that serves us now well
And the other in glory where we all want to dwell
Let's not forget the Oldtimers that started on time
Who parted the sod and rang the first chime
They just didn't know how well she'd stand the test of time

FAMILY TRILOGY: PART I

TO MY WIFE MARILYN
Keith Clifford

By me tonight a poem is born
After it's written it could draw scorn
But from my heart and pen it flows
Brought on by the weather and new-fallen snow
We live in Dakota, a hard land to know
The home of our loved ones, both now and long ago
It gave me riches beyond compare
Then left me wanting, it seemed not to care
I've lost my gold, silver and land
But it never could take my wife's loving hands
Hands that have helped me bad times to survive
Good times to savor, the tide to ride
She's tamed the garden, helped it grow
Canned and frozen so much you know
Family first, sunrise to dark
Always something, a new job to start
She'll find the time, somewhere to go
Well they need her help too, don't you know
But spring will come in Dakota land soon
Grass will turn green and the plants will grow
Then one early morning with coffee in hand
Out on the deck my Marilyn will stand
Then inside with a smile all happy and posed
She calls come look quick, there's a brand new rose
So Dakota is harsh and Dakota is grand
But I'll tell you one thing, she'll be tamed by Mom's loving hands
Love Keith

FAMILY TRILOGY: PART II

OUR AMY
Keith Clifford

A little girl at our house lives
She may never know the joy she gives
Until some day down the line
She has a little sweetheart just like mine
Her loving smile, her childish wit
Has done a lot for my life's trip
Although just nine it sometimes seems
She has so many older dreams
School she loves so very well
The math, the English and learning to spell
Her teachers praise her and this we see
By the wonderful papers she brings home to Ma and Me
She's oh so proud she learned to ride
A bike so young, you can just see the pride
And rollerskating when she can
She goes frontwards and backwards, man oh man
Helps in the garden and mows the lawn
Goes along to sales, loves to tag along
Sunday school pleases this little lass
Lots of times she's the only one in Mary's class
Picks up old bulletins, then the candles she lights
Then hurries back down to sit at Mom's right
So my dearest Amy, thought this poem I hope you see
Just how much you mean to your Mom and Me
                    Love Daddy

FAMILY TRILOGY: PART III

FOR OUR DAUGHTER AND NEW SON
Keith Clifford

When happy times to our lives come
It takes more people trying than just one
In this case it started out with two
And ended up here at Sterling Church with people in these pews
We're here today to see the Bride and Groom
And listen to vows taken in this Holy room
Promises made and rings put on
The smiles, the tears and laughter could go on till dawn
Arven and Carol and their families joined today
For a joyous trip through this life's stay
A new home started and changes for all
But with the love they have things will never stall
Arm in arm and hand in hand
The bigger the problem the taller they'll stand
So let's say a prayer that what started today
Will bless them all as they travel life's way
And united them in hearts and body and life
As they start this trip as Husband and Wife
      With all our love from Mom and Dad

Written October 15, 1986
Wedding November 1, 1986

Photo: Sinai Historical Committee

Dakota's Patriotism

This sign was erected on the west edge of Sinai for the 1976 Bicentennial celebration. O. B. Stime and Mrs. Jim Stimpson designed and built the sign which was erected by the Sinai 4-H Club.

TREAT THEM HORSES RIGHT
Gloria Dyc

In the heat of October
snakes trade off their lives
for a moment on warm pavement
and the sumac has reddened
in the hollows of the plains
Near an interstate cafe
three moose heads stare
from the top of a trailer
The careless laughter of the hunters
can be heard in the Murdo cafe
they must have travelled far north
to track a diminishing herd
The eyes of the moose
are congealed and vacant
their tongues hang as indignities
On the top of other trucks
antelope are stacked and tied
legs and necks entwined
Here there is no evidence
of the moose carcasses

Was the heart of the moose
consumed for strength?
The hide could be used to tie a drum
Will the flesh be dried for winter?
Will the horns be used in ceremony?
Sam Moves Camp tells this story:
He went hunting once
with a white man who shot a deer
The deer fell but the spirit lingered

Gloria Dyc has published poetry and fiction in numerous small press journals. She spent 10 years as the co-editor of *Moving Out*, a feminist publication. She has won a major award in fiction from the University of Michigan. Currently she is the Chair of the General Studies Department at Sinte Gleska College on the Rosebud Reservation.

"Shoot him again, this time for good"
Sam told his friend
Instead the man went to the lake
and submerged the deer's head
and watched the bubbles rise
"You don't do that"
that's what Sam said
But the hunter had no ears
a few weeks later
he was swept away in a flood

There was a man, Sam says
who was mean to horses
once his arm swelled up
hideous and twice its usual size
A woman healer was called in
she had the power
when she prayed a bird came to help
emerging out of her flesh
This bird pecked at his arm
and drew out a long hair
that hair was horse hair
And she said to that man
Treat them horses right
next time you mistreat horses
even I won't be able to help

Will the hunters end hollow as trees
consumed by diseases within?
One aberrant cell can cause a mutiny
What evidence of carelessness
will be found in their bonds?
And will the examiners be any wiser?

WITH IRON SHELL
ON THE WAY TO HIS GREAT-GREAT
GRANDFATHER'S GRAVE
Gloria Dyc

Wagon trails are still visible
faint branches off the main road
that leads to the bluff
where Mazaponkeska is buried
A rich doctor from Iowa
installed a headstone
where his remains rest
high above a timbered valley

> *My great-great grandfather*
> *had many wives*
> *and he loved children*
> *there'd never be orphans around*
> *he took them all into his band*
> *And he was brave*
> *once he killed eleven Pawnees*
> *My people were strong*

The people camped on these flats
Iron Shell remembers getting up
on cold mornings in a tent
his mother tending to the fire
It was a long hike to the road
where the school bus stopped
and behond that windbreak
Shit, it'd be cold
They were poor- -yes
still there was some labor
before the machines took over

All my people
they have this balding spot
on the top of their head
and these long braids
That's all you could see
these swinging braids

A few stones from a foundation
remain where a dance hall once stood
on weekends they'd rabbit dance
and they tried to square dance, too
there was homemade brew
thought they didn't drink much
They had sweat lodges
and the smoke from the fires
would draw the people together
to pray and visit one another

Once I was hunting
walking across here
I heard a wagon coming
the sound of hooves
a whip on horse flesh
And I thought
there are no wagons here
not anymore
And I just got out quick

Iron Shell wants to be buried
here close to his grandfather
On this land there is sandstone
it can be used in the sweatlodge
On this land there are willows
the bark is dried and smoked in a pipe

Photo: Cheryl Gorder
Winter scene: final resting place.

IN MEMORIAM

Leroy Iseminger

Leroy Iseminger is the pastor of the West Nidaros Lutheran Church in Crooks, SD. He relishes the beauty of the plains and can sit for hours beneath a cottonwood tree listening to the "evening breeze that broadcasts the euphony of the prairie."

The southwest mid-summer wind was blowing and the sun was about to set with a blazing benediction on the South Dakota prairie when the old pastor stopped on the rutted road on the gumbo hill that was above the little church and cemetery near the town that was no more. Years ago, it had been Van Metre, a village on the Bad River's gumbo sod. He would not go down to the cemetery tonight. To night he merely stopped to see if the tree and the church were still there. Tomorrow morning, before the prairie winds would blow again, he would go down there and sit by the tree and reminisce, and he would allow himself one more time to feel the kind of pain that is very far beyond words. Tomorrow, he would not be too busy being conscientious to notice it. He would go early when it would be quiet and still. She had hated the wind. She had often told them that. As he looked at the western sky, he reflected on his last trip to this place. It had been fifteen years. Tonight, it had seemed to be only yesterday. As he had gotten older, time went by so quickly. It does for anyone who lives under the threat of a sentence.

Fifteen years ago, almost to the day, he had come to this place. Why here? It was here that he had often come years before that. Here he had had the chance to convert his feelings of loneliness into solitude and had found

God entering into the emptiness of his heart. Here, because of the topography of this place, he had experienced a little bit of the desert and had visualized that the prairie is not only a dry place where people can die from thirst but also there in that vast empty space where there is nothing but prairie and sky is where the God of love can reveal himself and offer his promises. It had seemed that in this place, in this wilderness, in this emptiness, in the naked loneliness of it and in its quietness he could get in touch with his soul again. Nothing was here except the prairie's flowers and its winds to keep the grave stones in the cemetery and in his heart company. So many of the stones in the little church's cemetery marked children's graves. He had asked an attendant at a Memorial Day service why there were so many children's graves. The old rancher had told him in two words. His whisky-voice rasped the words, "Snake bit." Fifteen years ago the windows of the small church had been boarded up. By now, the boards would have weathered. That day there had been also a wind without rain. Tonight, he observed that there had been too many days like that again and the prairie was dry. It was used to that. That day, too, he had been lonely. Perhaps even more lonely than he had been on previous trips to this place. No one was there to be with him...only God and he needed Him that day, too.

Now today he was back. Back then, he had come to perform a committal service. Pastors are called upon at times to do that. The attendant at the gas station sixty miles down the road had noted his out-of-state license and had asked him, "What are you doing in these here parts?" "I have come to bury a butterfly. A creature as beautiful as a butterfly needs a decent burial." The attendant had looked at him strangely and then had talked about him to the other ranchers in the station after the old clergyman had driven away. Two of them had laughed. One had sent a mouthful of tobacco spit at the cuspidor. He missed it. It didn't matter.

"WHAT ARE YOU DOING IN THESE HERE PARTS?"

"I HAVE COME TO BURY A BUTTERFLY."

"I have come to bury a butterfly." It had been the symbol of their relationship. He had brought a little box with him which contained so much of their relationship...the letters...notes and carefully selected cards. The last item in the box was a butterfly comb that she had taken out of her hair and had given him on the night that she had had to say goodbye to him. He had also brought along a little cedar tree he had dug. It was native to the prairie and he hoped it would grow. Then, there would be something that would be living in the midst of all of the death in that place. An old English proverb said, "He that plants trees loves others besides himself." He had. On that night she had asked him to bury her. She had told him he had to do that. He could not. To have done that would have been to have buried a part of him. That he would not do. "Next Thursday you have a funeral for Mrs. Balstrom. Put me in her grave, too. You're a pastor. You can do that."

That day, fifteen years ago, he had come to bury a butterfly and to get back in touch with his soul and with his life and with his God. Then, he had dug a hole. It had to be deep enough, but could it ever be deep enough? The first things he had put into it were all of the letters and notes and cards--reminders that man shall not live by bread alone, but by the word...During the coming years those buried words would nourish the cedar tree above them as they had nourished him. They would give life as they had given life. The gift that was most difficult to place in the little grave had been her comb.

On that morning he had not kept back the tears, and only the prairie had heard him cry. His teacher at the Seminary in that Grief class had often said, "Time doesn't heal a thing...it is not unusual for a real gain in working through the feelings of the loss-experience to be achieved only to be wiped out by the return of an acute attack of grief which was triggered by an occurence or experience somehow related to the original loss." Not only had he underlined the sentence in the class text, but it had been underlined in his life as well. His hands had crushed the gumbo clods into powder- -enough to gently cover the comb. On top of it all, he had placed the cedar tree. His grandfather had taught him how to plant a cedar tree when he had been a small boy. "Always tie a string on the north branch and plant it the way it had been growing, son."

He had come this day because he remembered the butterfly and he now wanted to see if the tree was alive. He should have known that it would be, for after all, buried beneath its roots was that which would help give it life. On the day he planted the tree, it had seemed that God had reassured him that He would watch over the tree in a special way. He looked again in the direction of the orange sky. It seemed that he could see some other little cedar trees growing. He wasn't sure, but he remembered what his grandfather had told him: "Get one started, son, and the birds will carry its seeds and plant cedars all over." Tomorrow he would count them when he stood by the old cedar tree. He knew he would weep again. And that would be right. That would be just right. He would not stop the tears. Nor would he try. It had been she who had helped teach him how right it was to express feelings and to know what a friendship beyond birthdays could mean.

Tomorrow he would repeat his gratitude for the butterfly. It had been on loan to him from God...a gift of grace. Friendships are gifts. He remembered a saying on a plaque:

> *People so seldom say, "I love you,"*
> *And then it's either too late*
> *or love goes*
> *So when I tell you*
> *I love you*
> *It doesn't mean*
> *I know you'll never go*
> *Only that I wish*
> *you didn't have to.*

Tomorrow would be the last time he would come to this place- -this special place. His diseased legs would soon be removed. He had been fortunate to retain them as long as he had. While he stood there in the twilight, a pair of prairie grouse rose out of the buffalo grass and flew towards the river. A meadowlark sang its evening vespers a cappella from a rotting fence post. It didn't seem to mind that there was only one in the audience. Two prairie dogs barked at each other and a mother killdeer ran down the road with cocked wings. The old pastor was overcome with a feeling of awe. For a brief moment he knew it didn't make any difference he was going to die. For a little while, he belonged to that beauty and everything was as it should be.

He got into his car, turned it around and drove away. He did not turn on the radio. He did not have to do that in order to hear the music. He could hear it faintly, distinctly. It was the kind of music which, at one time, a butterfly had seemed to sing to him. But, too soon, the songs had all gone off the air and he drove on in the silence that had always been a part of his life.

TIM GIAGO

Tim Giago is the editor and publisher of the reservation-based *Lakota Times* of Martin, South Dakota. The *Lakota Times* is the largest Indian-owned weekly newspaper in the United States. Mr. Giago is the founder of the newspaper which serves fourteen Indian reservations in three states.

Born on the Pine Ridge Indian Reservation to parents of the Oglala Sioux Tribe, Tim's Oglala Sioux name is Nanwica Kciji, which means "Defender". He has lived up to this name through his extensive writing, in which he aims to educate the non-Indian public of the issues affecting today's Indian population.He does so by writing which contains razor-sharp criticism at times, and tongue-in-cheek humor at other times, but always with an interest in improving the way the non-Indian public deals with Indians. His general attitude can be summed up in his own words, "Open your eyes and at the same time you may open your heart."

His writing has appeared in many national newspapers, and currently his weekly syndicated column appears in sixteen newspapers, including the Phoenix *Gazette* and the Minneapolis *Star-Tribune*. He has written two books: *Aboriginal Sin* and *Notes From Indian Country*. He is also the founder and first president of the Native American Press Association, a position which he presently holds.

His writing has won him national awards and attention, including the H. L. Mencken writing award in 1985, a very prestigious award for journalists.In 1982 he won the Media Person of the Year Award at the American Indian Media Conference in Albuquerque.

Mr. Giago was educated at Pine Ridge, SD, San Jose, CA, and the University of Nevada. He served in the US Navy from 1952 to 1958. He is married and his wife Linda is the business manager of the newspaper.

The following three selections are from his syndicated column, which he also calls "Notes From Indian Country."

TIME TO ENJOY TIME

Notes From Indian Country

Syndicated Column

March 14, 1986

Tim Giago (Nanwica Kciji)

Time never challenged the Indian or worked against him as an enemy to be feared. Time was for silently marking the passing of the seasons. It was a thing to be enjoyed.

The full moon that crossed the night skies from horizon to horizon indicated the months of the year. For instance, during the month when the air became so frigid it caused the twigs and branches of the trees to make popping sounds (late December and early January to the white man) was called "The Moon of Popping Trees" by the Lakota (Sioux) people.

There was no single day, such as March 21, that told the Indian that this was the first day of spring. When the tender young grass pushed its way up through the fertile soil, and the geese, ducks, and whooping cranes sang their songs as they traveled North, this told the Indian that the season of new beginnings was here.

As the white man made his way West, he brought along a clock. The Indian observed the white man as he geared his entire existence around the movement of the hands on the face of the clock.

The various Indian agents assigned to the different tribes by the federal government would become infuriated when strict adherence to time was not followed by the Indian people.

When an agent called for a meeting to take place at 10 a.m. sharp, he expected the participants to show up on time. To the Indian, as long as he made it sometime during the day, he saw nothing wrong. The white agents soon began to say that the tribes operated on Indian time.

Unfairly, Indian time became synonymous with laziness, never mind that the Indian usually arose at the crack of dawn to greet the morning sun in prayer to his Creator.

As the Indian tribes came under control of the Bureau of Indian Affairs, and as the tribal governments organized under federal regulations and federal funds, the chains that bound the white man to the clock began to envelop the individual Indian.

Eight hours of work for eight hours of pay became the rule. The people that needed to visit the governmental offices to take care of business knew that if they did not make it there during the prescribed business hours, they would be left out in the cold.

In return, the grass roots Indian people expected that if the tribal or BIA employees were being paid a salary to serve them, they had to be at their desks and available, especially since many of the residents of the large Indian reservations had to travel many miles over unpaved roads to reach the agency headquarters.

As the tribes began to rely more and more upon their own resources to survive financially, they also embraced the concept that time is money and money is time. If a tribal employee was being paid to put in a 40-hour week, he was expected to earn that pay and put in his 40 hours. Time clocks soon began to appear on the walls of the tribal administration walls.

I've listened to many elderly white people talk about a time in their lives when life was more simple. They recall those days of their youth nostalgically and wonder what the world is coming to.

I remember a slogan I heard quite often as a young man. It was a slogan one usually saw at the theater, on the big screen, just before the main feature. "Time marches on" said a voice asking for contributions to The March of Dimes fund to find a cure for polio.

Time marches on. Just as the world has been made small by satellites and mass communications, so too has the concept of Indian time shrunk to fit the times.

Don't be sad. To the Indian all life is a circle. We are born, we live, and then we die. In the old ways of the Lakota, the body that had been nourished by feeding upon the four-legged, the winged, and the fish, was placed on a scaffold high on a hill, and given back to the creatures that had sustained it life.

DEEP DOWN, MOST INDIANS STILL DO NOT ALLOW TIME TO DICTATE TO THEM, THEY STILL FIND THE TIME TO ENJOY TIME.

The Indian does not live in a vacuum. Just as the world around us has changed, we have had to change in order to survive.

Perhaps time has taken on a new meaning to the Indian tribes of this land, but so has the will to survive.

Whenever we are late for work or for a meeting, we still joke that we are "operating on Indian time." This gives us a brief respite from the rigidity that has been forced upon us by circumstance.

Deep down, most Indians still do not allow time to dictate to them. They still find the time to enjoy time.

Photo: Cheryl Gorder

The First Annual Indian Exposition in Rapid City, July 11-13, 1987, was a colorful and entertaining event. All people are invited to pow-wows to have a good time. There are different kinds of events, including lots of competition dancing. The competitors have breathtaking costumes in traditional and contemporary styles.

INDIANS JUST WANT TO BE THEMSELVES

Notes From Indian Country

Syndicated Column

May 9, 1986

Tim Giago (Nanwica Kciji)

©1986 *Lakota Times* reprinted with permission

Joseph James is an Eskimo living in Anchorage, Alaska. One day while he was reading the January issue of *National Geographic Magazine* , he nearly jumped to his feet.

James sat down that day and wrote a letter to the *Tundra Times,* a newspaper owned by Eskimo Indian, Aleut Publishing Company, a corporation of Alaska natives headed by Sylvia Carlsson.

When James left out the words of certain words in one passage of the article he was very upset by what it said. Here is the passage:

"The major issue is land rights...the issue has pitted the state not so much against the natives as it has against the federal government.

"It is the policy of government to return traditional Aboriginal lands to the people. To prevent that from happening...We are looking at ways and means right now of legally stopping the frightening prospect of aggregation of aboriginal land...

"What the federal government wants to do is give control of the whole northern coastline to Aboriginals. How do we defend our country, or keep exotic diseases out, if white people are denied access to our northern coastlines?

"It is not that the government is insensitive to the needs of the Aboriginal people. But rather than helping them make their own way in society, the policy is one of paternalism."

The point James wanted to make is that it was not the American Indians of America that were being discussed. Instead, it was the native peoples of Australia. He had deliberately omitted Australian names, proper nouns, etc., to show that the Australian Aborigines were going through the same heartbreaking problems faced by Native Americans.

James summed up his bitter feelings with, "Does every inch of ground, every blade of grass, everything the white man stands upon, even for a moment, automatically belong to him? Is there some divine right the white men have over the entire world?"

This letter by James is important because is focuses upon a point that many Indians are trying to get across to the dominant society. In the lectures I give at various universities I try to include it as food for thought. The United States government has failed to assimilate American Indians into the mainstream because Indians do not want to be drowned in the "Great Melting Pot."

The point James was attempting to make, and the point that I make when I speak, is that we (Indians) are different. Being different does not make us wrong, it does not make us anti-American, less patriotic, or enemies of the white people. It simply means that we are different and we see nothing wrong in this. What is more, we do not want to be like the white man.

*BEING DIFFERENT DOES NOT MAKE US WRONG,
IT DOES NOT MAKE US ANTI-AMERICAN, LESS
PATRIOTIC, OR ENEMIES OF THE WHITE PEOPLE.
WE BELIEVE WE CAN BE DIFFERENT AND STILL
BE FRIENDS TO THE WHITE MAN*

We believe we can be different and still be friends to the white man. After all, isn't the United States friendly with other nations of the Third World that are different?

The North and South American continents are dotted with many Third World developing nations. Whether they are called reservations, reserves, pueblos, rancheros, or corporations (as is the case in Alaska), they are independent and sovereign nations.

James emphasized this point with: "I no longer want their equal rights nor to become white like them. I only want to be myself: Native, separate, different, and all the things the white man says aren't good for me, like our owns laws, our own customs, our own government, our own schools, our own way of life, our own land, and no white man inventing laws to take it all away again."

James makes this point very powerfully in his final sentence: "Do you understand me gussak? Read my lips: **I DO NOT WANT TO BE LIKE YOU.**"

As American Indians we know that there is change in the air and that for us to survive as a distinct race of people, we must change in certain ways. But basically, we are Indian, we were born Indian, and most of us will die Indian.

At one time in history the white man ruled over every continent on this planet, but no more. Other nations have discovered something the American Indian has known for centuries: they are different and they want to stay that way.

CECILIA FIRE THUNDER
PLAINS INDIAN DOLLS·OGLALA SIOUX

Photo: Cheryl Gorder

Cecelia Fire Thunder, maker of Plains Indian dolls, is also a competition dancer and is actively involved in women's issues. Here she displays her dolls at the Indian Exposition in Rapid City.

INDIANS AND THE MASS MEDIA

Notes From Indian Country

Syndicated Column

July 3, 1986

Tim Giago (Nanwica Kciji)

To the white-owned mass media, Indians are objects to be written about and viewed, but not to be heard from: out of sight, out of mind.

Indians are people living in teepees, wearing buckskin clothing and sporting eagle feathers in their hair. They are imitated by children whooping around the house emulating the "Hollywood" misconception of Indians.

Indians are subjects for quaint and unusual stories that hit the wires and are picked up nationally. Indians are people to be pitied and wept over. We are either the Noble Savage or the downtrodden loser.

Cursed with our own brand of radicals, who have managed to set us back by about 50 years, we have been rolled into one bundle. We are expected to remain as we were 200 years ago by the weeping liberals who think we cannot progress along with the times without becoming something they cannot readily identify as Indian.

There are more federal agencies regulating Indian tribes than any other ethnic group on the continent. Most of what we own on our reservation is held in trust by the Bureau of Indian Affairs through its parent agency, the U.S. Department of Interior. The only problem with this arrangement is that Indians are expected to provide all of the trust.

Self-appointed spokesmen and fraudulent medicine men travel about the country passing themselves off as the real McCoy contributing to the prevailing myths and misconceptions about the First Americans.

Long ago the blacks had the political clout to get grade B movies demeaning blacks removed from the archives of the major television networks. If the movies were considered to be classics, they were edited to remove the racial overtones.

The Indian has not been so lucky. Since we are small in numbers our cries of indignation to the movie industry have fallen on deaf ears. As a result a new generation of Indian haters and people ignorant about what it is an Indian is all about has been spawned.

What is even more terrible, the grade B movies filled with so many errors and untruths about Indians are now being accepted as fact by this new generation.

COLUMBUS DAY IS A DAY OF MOURNING ON MANY INDIAN RESERVATIONS.

Indians are the only race of people on this continent that are distinguished by blood quantum. Have you ever heard a black man referred to as a half-breed? Has any other minority been forced to abide by regulations affecting his education, health, and welfare upon his degree of blood?

White newspapers still refer to Indian women as squaws, a word despised by the Indian women themselves. Indian males are still refereed to as bucks or braves.

Indians are still useds as mascots for high school, college and professional sports teams. We have the Washington Redskins, Cleveland Indians, the Redmen of St. Johns, and the Atlanta Braves to name just a few. Why don't we have the Minnesota Whitemen or the Washington Black-skins?

The opinion pages of most daily newspapers carry few opinion columns written by minorities. The great melting pot has become so homogeneous, at least in the myopic views of white editorial page editors, that a voice not in tune with the majority choir is a voice that will never be given an opportunity to be heard.

That is too bad. Most Americans will never learn the things that could be taught to them by the American Indian, or at least they won't learn it from their local newspaper.

The First Americans look at this country through a different prism than other Americans. Accepted symbols of democracy like the Statue of Liberty and the carvings on Mount Rushmore do not mean the same thing to Native Americans as they do to other Americans.

American Indians can see America through the facade presented to the rest of the world. We can see the warts right along with the beauty spots.

White America is denying itself the opportunity to look at itself through the eyes of the oldest race of people in this hemisphere by not allowing the opinions of Native Americans to stand right alongside of the liberal and conservative views of its white columnists.

Many American holidays don't mean the same thing to Indians as they do to the general population. For instance, Columbus Day is a day of mourning on many Indian reservations.

JOHN KENNEDY: "OF ALL AMERICANS, THE AMERICAN INDIAN IS THE LEAST UNDERSTOOD AND THE MOST MISUNDERSTOOD."

In 1960, President John F. Kennedy said, "Of all Americans, the American Indian is the least understood and the most misunderstood."

Twenty-six years later, nothing has really changed.

While growing up on an Indian reservation, I was taught to believe that America was strong because of its diversity. Faced with the closed minds and the closed doors at so many newspapers and television stations when it came to airing the opinions of Native Americans, I cannot help but believe that America will open its media doors only to those who think, act, and behave as they are expected to behave by the white editors and producers of the opinion pages and news stories.

In my mind, this is America's tragedy, and this is America's loss.

TO OUR SON, RAND
Bernette Rogenes

Lest you forget
The plains of Dakota
The valley...the rolling hills.
The coming of summer
And air crisp as apples
When the wheat's head fills.
The meadowlarks welcome
From an old fence post
The bright blue sky overhead
With fleecy white clouds riding high
And a soft green grass for a bed.
The crunchy snow, a sea of white
Studded with diamonds ona winter's night
The autographs of bird and beast
The paths of ski and sled
These are Dakota's memories
Lest you forget!
Lest you forget!

This poem was written when my son left
North Dakota after graduation from the
University of North Dakota.

Bernette Rogenes is the daughter of pioneers who
arrived in Dakota Territory in 1886. Their hard-
ships, plus the prodding of her eldest daughter,
caused her to write two books, *Coffee Time* and *My
Valley*. These books are a panoramic saga of the
Red River Valley of North Dakota which Bernette
loves so much. The books are enormously successful and are in second and third printings! Bernette's
other writing includes freelance articles for newspapers and magazines and a bimonthly column for
county newspapers. She is a "young" 72 and plans
to continue writing and sharing her heritage with
others.

Agnes Brewer

Agnes Brewer's poetry has strong insights into the native American view of life, and for obvious reasons. She was raised on land that had previously been part of the Yankton Sioux Reservation, and before that, tribal land. Her husband, now deceased, was part Sioux. She now lives in Yankton and serves people well by being a counselor in the field of Chemical Dependency.

Agnes is a visual artist as well as a poet. All of her artistic expressions show universal emotions, the king of feelings that everyone has.

Mary Goings

Mary Goings writes about the things she is most familiar with—the people she loves, her work, and her studies. She does not write "peaches and cream" poetry, but rather strives to write about social issues. She is involved with many people, mostly the poor and minorities, and she tries to deal with the harsh realities of their lives, but to do it in a style that can be called beautiful.

Mary says, "Writing poetry is a challenge to translate the abstraction of visions into the kind of feeling language that does not sacrifice those elusive creative qualities which first engendered them." Much of her poetry reflects her late husband's Sioux Indian heritage.

She has recently put together a series of poems, *Aries Rising,* to accompany to an anti-nuclear exhibition.

Although a Denver native, Mary has lived in South Dakota since 1942.

Agnes Brewer and Mary Goings are the poets who wrote the beautiful little book of poetry called *Womansight.* They deal with serious and important themes in life and handle these topics with expertise. The book is available from Blue Bird Publishing or from the poets. The next several poems are from these talented poets.

ARROWS
Agnes Brewer

Arrow feathers
hang limp and bedraggled,
gathering dust.
Old times will not return.
The buffalo
are confined to state parks;
never again to run free,
and the taste of their flesh
is in a tourist's mouth.

Wind still blows the prairie grass
and ruffles my hair, grown grey.
My heart ages...
and I long for
bright
straight arrows.

GOD-LUST

Agnes Brewer

The people desire to worship...
                    and the people yearn for a god.

Ever lusting after the life-source,
straining our hearts for a glimpse of the non-world,
so consumed with our own mortality
that the purpose of living's forgotten.
Generations have carried the search...
year after year have gods risen and fallen,
to sink in the limbo of man's spent illusion.

It has been said that there are no absolutes...
but men desire a person god.
                    Those who say not, lie.

Is the way to the life-source simple?
Are we blind?
Divergent ways swamp us,
the dusts of myriad minds clog our eyes.
The jottings on stone, venerated by dig-men,
are no more than jot
for they lead to a grave
and a museum shelf.

How long has it been
since a new god was born,
or new ones fashioned from old?
Through time after time
runs a second hand god,
dressed in new clothes
and a fresh coat of paint.

God, are you there?
Can you blame us, god?
We look at debris of the ages,
and question the cause of ancient god-passion.
Passion born of desire for life,
wanting to live forever...

not wanting to die forever.
Insupportable.
Unendurable.

Did we invent you,
for comfort in our insecurity?
Or did you plant god-seek in us?
A seek that becomes slashing pain,
ever recurring fear,
that surpasses love...
that suppresses love...

We can count from the earth-mother...
count to the virgin.
Eons of gods,
ages of goddesses.
Diverse heavens,
hell upon hell.
Love based or hate bared,
count final,
count fear.

This is not the age of faith;
an age hard to live in.
To be cradled in the arms of belief,
be it blind,
is to be longed for...
to be sought for.
The cold bed of the skeptic
grows colder with age;
as blood-heat starts to recede,
as the life-spark withdraws to its source;
then man reaches out for a god,
grasping and clutching,
with sighing heart.

Touch us, O life-source,
leave us not in our meanderings...
O please...

GROWTH-TIME
Agnes Brewer

Wind, water, rock, rain,
intertwined forces...
touching, speaking,
to the life-forms of earth.

The winds across rivers blow stong,
fingering freely.

The sky shimmers grey with
its lacings of silver light.

Blood glows and sap surges
for growth-time is here.

Father, sun...
energizing, calling forth life
by the radiance of sun-sperm,
interlocking with earth-mother sources,
revitalziing dormant earth-genes;
caressing, coaxing, then, willing
the new emanation of life.

Come my earth-brothers,
let us not fight these forces external
for the call on our powers internal
and answer we must.

How difficult to make one's way
Along the paths we mortals trod
When one would rather step among the stars
And walk with God!

LULLABYE
Mary Goings

Mamma, I'm hungry...give me some bread?
Hush, Child, man's gone to the moon.
I'm hungry Mamma. What does it mean to be dead?

The wind's blowing, Mamma, and I'm so cold.
Hush, Child...man's gone to the moon.
Mamma, you're tired and your face looks so old.

Why did Johnny go, Mamma? Why did he go?
Hush, Child. Man's gone to the moon.
Why, Mamma, why? We all loved him so.

"Feed me, Mamma, feed me," that's what he said.
Hush, Child, man's gone to the moon.
You're crying again, Mamma...your face is all red.

I'm so hungry, Mamma. Why is there nothing to eat?
Hush, Child...man's gone to the moon.
Only some milk, Mamma? Some bread? Maybe some meat?

I'm so tired, Mamma, and it's not even night.
Hush, Child. Man's gone to the moon.
Why do I feel sleepy, Mamma? So sleepy and light?

Oh, I want to play, Mamma....to run...and have fun.
Hush, Child...Man's gone to the moon.
Where did the sun go, Mamma? *Where is the sun?*

Rest in Peace, Child.
                Man's gone to the moon!

WELFARE: THE RAGGED EDGE
Mary Goings

I am seared by all that I have seen
thick scars wrinkle my heart
I cannot write

The moon weeping through the window
cries my agonizing tears
in the argent glory of its light

I am numb
I cannot feel
their pain   my pain
is far too deep
buried in muscles and bones
dried-up breasts
the feet of shoeless children
and the plight of crippled old men
walking in the pouring rain

in a flickering flight of breath
the wind carries my wounds

I cannot catch the words

THE ARTIFACT
Mary Goings

An ancient relic sits alone: a Prize
ensconced within a used museum case
luminous under glare of bullet lights
that emphasize the markings on that vase.

Fashioned by a skillful master's hand
it mutely witnessed prehistoric days;
now, puzzled scholars spend their time
deciphering the riddles of its clays

and those of other roughened shards unearthed
beside a river's edge, so deep, in fact
dubious viewers wonder while shaking heads
how that lone vessel remained intact.

Still others ponder how that lustrous pot,
devoid of feeling, lacking speech or sight,
unthinking, embracing only air survived
indifferent to the crunching of time's slow bite

while its maker, so expert at his task
is gone. Were the coals that much hotter?
His idiot of clay, some chancey mix?
What? That the pot should so outlast the potter.

THE AUCTION
Mary Goings

I bought a lovely
piece of someone's
life this August
afternoon. Don't quite
know how it fits in
with chairs and beds
and pots and pans
TVs dressers quilts
and stoves, but there
it was- -glistening
in the sun
brightly
as her tears

EPILOGUE
Mary Goings

How difficult to make one's way
Along the paths we motrals trod
When one would rather step among the stars
And walk with God!

DAKOTA WELCOME

By Lorna L. Steckler

Lorna L. Steckler based this story on fact, from information handed down to her by her mother, Alma Bancroft Mullen. Lorna also writes poetry, paints, and is working on a historical romantic novel. She lives in Vermillion and at 64 years of age is learning the joy of mastering computer word processing.

"We can always turn back," Mary offered weakly, fighting to hold back her tears. Her usual sweet smile was failing badly in trying to hide her trembling chin. Mary bit her lower lip to halt the quiver.

"Maybe it's better than it looks." Delos was grumbling as her halted his team of oxen. His eyes squinted as they took in this dismal scene before them. "Well, here we are in the Territorial Capitol." It appeared that her husband was speaking to no one in particular and in a sympathetic gesture, Mary placed one small hand upon her tired husband's arm. Delos covered it with his own rough palm and gave her slender fingers a gentle squeeze.

The rut-filled, muddy streets of Yankton welcomed this small, straggly train of wagons to its dreary journey's end.

It was early September, 1869. There had been eleven wagons at the beginning of the trip west. A few parted from the group and followed another route that took them through areas along the Platte River.

Today, only seven had pulled their families and all they owned into this growing settlement with the land agency.

The long, hard venture was over, or had it just begun? Delos Bancroft wondered why on earth he had fought so hard against making the trip by rail. He knew why. They, like the others, had brought almost everything they owned with them. They bought the best cattle. They bought mules or oxen to pull their small wagons because they were loaded with precious cargo. They needed to bring a few pieces of furniture; one of the most important being his wife's genuine Isaac M. Singer sewing machine. Howe had really invented the first but it was Singer who put the foot treadle and the pressure foot to hold the "goods" down on the plate. Mary couldn't get along without hers now. Delos had sold them and it was one of the few costly items he had purchased for his wife, unless he counted the pretty, china tea service he gave her one time for Christmas. It was to take the place of one she had in England. It had belonged in the family many years and was pure silver. Her mother was forced to sell it in order to bury her little brother after her died. This was soon after they arrived in America. Her father had died some months before they sailed.

Delos smiled to himself as he though about his small wife. She really didn't fit into this picture out here on the plains. She had been tutored and brought up to live the life of a lady. Her mother had left the estate manor rather hastily. Some things she left behind and others she sold in order to purchase passage for herself and the two children. She did manage to bring the silver service and it had come in handy and brought a tidy sum when they needed it badly at her young son's death. The service had been precious to her only because it was an heirloom and handed down in her family. Mary's brother had always been frail and after a few months in America, he worsened. Nothing could be done for him.

Mary told the story often to Delos. When they had children of their own, she was pleased that her husband wished to name one of their sons after her brother, Thomas Harsden and her father Sir Thomas.

"I will always call him Marsden! Sure do love that boy. He ain't much of a boy since he ran off to join the 3rd Wisconsin Calvary. He fought in the Volunteers because his brother died in that dark, Civil War."

Delos was thinking aloud but others could not hear him well. He and Mary did have a lad who died at the Battle of Pittsburg Landing. It upset Marsden so that he ran off to join and get into the action. He had been much too young but he remained until he was mustered out in 1865. He then joined a group of surveyors going to Colorado.

He was gone many years. Mary thought him dead also but now was beside herself with joy because he came home and joined the journey to Dakota with the Maxons, the Cross family and the Bancrofts!

Cross, the preacher, was strict with his girls. Had to be! He was a learned man and later on a member of the 1879-1880 Territorial Legislature. He was deeply religious but was usually involved with something of a political nature. He was a good man and father to his young daughters but he missed his wife dearly. He had married her back in Wisconsin in 1860. She had been a beautiful young woman. She gave birth to several children and after each became more frail. P. N. knew that Emma was not a strong woman, even as a young girl. Her parents had told him this. He had decided not to come west to Dakota because of this but Emma knew her family would be and she wanted P. N. and his own family to also.

Philetus gave in to Emma but he was having a time of it now. Emma took ill and her condition was so grave that she died at the very beginning of the trip. The trail was difficult and it wore on her strength.

The Cross sons had their own wagons. They drove theirs up ahead of the others. They were good lads. One had a wife and now, a baby on the way. They helped the best they could but the little girls needed the female touch. P. N. was sometimes astounded at the tasks his eldest daughter could do. P. N. would have to keep an eye on her. The lads were beginning to notice Alice. She appeared to be more mature than she really was. He felt a little guilty that her time had to be taken up with the care of the family at such a tender age.

It was over. Emma was gone. The trail so hard that it was easy for that consumption to kill her as it had others. They buried her in a sheltered spot with a young tree and a small rock as a marker.

Delos smiled again to himself as he though about the eldest of P. N.'s daughters. Cross had sons but they were older and had their wagon with plans of their own for the future. They were little help to their father but Alice made up for everything. She took over where their mother had been. She cooked, sewed, watched over her younger sisters like a mother hen and Marsden watched with great interest. He appeared to be quite taken with her.

Delos, thinking aloud softly, again: "Boyd, the scout, had done a fine job. He had turned out to be dependable and we are lucky to have hired him on for the trip."

Delos heard the sick wail of little Frank on the cot in the wagon. Frank's parents were dead. His own mother at Frank's birth and then his father took ill and died form consumption en route to Dakota. There was nobody to take care of Frank and Mary could hardly wait to bed him down in the Bancroft wagon. He had been so ill but in spite of the pathetic sound coming from behind Delos, Frank was improving with

Mary's tender care. "Looks like he is ours! I am getting a little old to raise a youngun like him but if Mary loves him, I can do it for her. Seems like a nice lad and he could be a great help with my blacksmithing and carpentry work if the land does not work out. I am not a farmer but I can learn."

Delos stared vacantly out into the dark, unpleasant day. He was so deep in thought that he vaguely heard the laughter coming from the settlers on the corner. He turned to watch the men gathered there. They appeared to be in good spirits. Delos was not familiar with this climate. He did not know what many others who already worked land nearby had learned. They knew that tomorrow could dawn as a bright, sunny day and a full breeze could turn to dust, the muddy street where the wagons were mired in deep ruts.

Delos handed the reins to Mary but reminded her with some tenderness, to stay inside the wagon for warmth. He jumped, and found that his heavy, leather boots sank deep into muck. He was stiff and sore from the trip and weather. He was close to sixty and groaned slightly as he made his way toward the wooden walk. He motioned to his son Marsden in the next wagon, to follow. Marsden hurried to his side and they both stepped up on the corner at the same time.

The settlement had but a very few buildings of size and all were crucial to its development. The town was growing rapidly and now was beginning to be a center for river trade and showed great promise. The bleak appearance betrayed the prosperity as it was just starting to enjoy its business advantages. It was the major outfitting point for the Black Hills. Many caravans or single wagons started farther westward from there.

"It is the Capitol of Dakota Territory! This place will go down in the history books."

That small settlement near the ferry landing at Vermillion looked as though it could use a good blacksmith or a man with carpentry training and Delos had experience in both. By trade, he was a tinsmith and silversmith but had turned to the shoeing of horses to make some money. He had learned the art of repairing sewing machines and had sold some of the new models in Wisconsin. Everybody had horses. He could always find work making horseshoes and working in iron. Mary wanted him to own land and had prodded him in this new venture.

"I hope I don't disappoint her. I have never farmed a piece of land in my life. I have done a good many things. I worked with my father on the Erie canal and I am mightly proud of that, but working the land out here on the plains is different and I am getting on in years! Is it possible an old dog can learn new tricks out here with the Indians and a whole new way of life? I have to make a go of it! I was afraid to travel out here from Wisconsin by ourselves. I would never have decided to try if that group hadn't made up a small train. Many came out in "single" wagons now but it was a very hard trip and some didn't make it."

The Bancrofts had settled in Wisconsin after coming that far from Cheery Valley, New York. The Cross family had lived in Wisconsin for some time but P. N. had been born in Ohio. His father, also Philetus N. was born in Ohio but moved his family to Wisconsin early on. His son, P. N. took up government land in Clay County. He cultivated and improved his one hundred and sixty acres from when he arrived in 1869, to 1883, when he decided to sell. Grasshoppers, the foods, and pioneer hardship took its toll. He was interested in politics and became active in it. He had a strong faith and was a preacher at heart and spent many years as an evangelistic minister. He wore a long, full beard and was rarely seen without his Bible. He gave his eldest daughter to Thomas Marsden Bancroft.

All of what happened to the Cross family and Maxons and the Bancrofts, before they arrived in Yankton, and all that was to come about, was extremely important to Delos as he searched the future with a troubled mind.

"Whatever is beyond this settlement, must be what my Mary calls infinity!" Delos was muttering again.

"Did you speak, father?"

"Just thinking aloud again, son."

Delos kept turning those and other sobering thoughts over in his mind but he made an effort and his words came out reassuringly.

"Sure is an exciting time to be alive, isn't it son? Just look at all the people who have faith in a future out here! I sure hope we can get a piece of land close to that little town of Vermillion! Wonder where that Land Office is located? Must be that building over there!"

Marsden didn't hear him, he was thinking about Alice Cross, the young woman he wanted to marry. "I'll have to wait a few years. She is only a young girl but seems much older because she is mature for her age. I guess that comes when you have to take over the raising of your smaller sisters."

Alice Cross was at that moment, kneeling in prayer. She thanked the Lord for bringing them safely and asked Him to watch over her mother Emma who had died. She had her small sisters, Clara, Nell and Eva bow their heads. Their mother had been Emma Maxon.

The Maxons were busy finishing tasks the head of the family had asked of them.

Mary sat shivering, more from excitement than the cool, damp air. She pulled her shawl about her and glanced back into the wagon at little Frank.

Philetus N. Cross? He stood erectly, firmly holding his Bible underneath his left arm. He stroked his magnificent beard, then as another man walked away, he took his place. First in the line at the Land Office, was the "preacher."

"Welcome to Dakota Territory, sir!"

Photo: Cheryl Gorder

The Bushnell Bash, in the tiny town of Bushnell, South Dakota, is an annual celebration that includes exhibits of artists and craftsmen, as well as as a parade and special activities. This covered wagon was special to the bicentennial celebration of 1976 and showed how typical pioneers arrived in the territory.

Dakota Christmas!
Photos: Cheryl Gorder

AUDRAE VISSER
South Dakota's Poet Laureate

Teacher, writer, international traveler, genealogist, photographer, librarian. All of these describe South Dakota's poet laureate.

Audrae was born at Hurley, South Dakota into a home of Dutch-Scotch-Irish background. She attended rural schools and graduated from Flandreau High School. She majored in botany as an undergraduate and in librarianship as a graduate student. She received her M.A. from the University of Denver.

Audrae has taught in South Dakota, Minnesota, and Japan. She has been an English teacher and librarian in addition to her poetry writing..

Her poetry writing began in the seventh grade, and by the time she was a senior in high school, she was published in *Senior Scholastic,* a national high school magazine. Her poetry has appeared in *Pasque Petals, American Sonnets and Lyrics, Prairie Poets, Voices of South Dakota, Prize Poems of the National Federation of State Poetry Societies* & *Laurel Leaves,* the national official publication of the United Poets International.

She became South Dakota's poet laureate in 1974 when Governor Richard Kneip gave her the appointment. She is a member of the United Poets International as well as other poetry and educaitonal organizations.

Her books are *Rustic Roads, Poems for Brother Donald, Meter for Momma, Poetry for Pop, South Dakota* & *Country Cousin,* from which the following selections have been chosen. She also penned a collection of whimsical short stories called *Honyocker Stories.*

Audrae's biography can be found in the prestigious publications *International Who's Who in Poetry, International Authors & Writer's Who's Who, Personalities of the West & Midwest, Who's Who in American Women, Who's Who in the Midwest,* & *Who's Who of North American Poets.*

Audrae presently resides in Elkton, and people interested in obtaining copies of her books may write to her at 710 Elk Street, Elkton SD 57026.

DEATH OF AN OLD FARMER

Audrae Visser

Out of this sunlit world you went today

Into that other world of peace and dark;

The wrens still trill their songs, the farm dogs bark,

The air smells good with new alfalfa hay- -

All the things you loved- -but you have gone away.

Your spirit like a run-down clock, now stark,

Refused another winding; thus we mark

Your end, which science can no longer stay.

Were you a humble man? You were not rich

Nor ruled those realms where high intriguings lurk- -

And yet, I'd say you were a man of wealth;

In your life you had your own respected niche,

And friends, a wife and children, honest work,

And almost to the end, your priceless health.

SOUTH DAKOTA

Audrae Visser

From sea to land as ten thousand years ticked past,
This state of ours emerged to greet the sky.
The restless waters left, and earth appeared.
Then came a vegetation lush and vast
Where dinosaurs could browse in plants neck-high
Until at last the air cooled off and cleared- -
Swamps dried, and "thundering lizards" were no more.
Gone were their heavy steps and awesome roar.
Now came the mile-deep glaciers, carving out
Missouri's river basin, leaving rocks
And long moraines and beds of rich black dirt.
Sea bottom slowly turned to prairie plains,
Where bison grazed in wide earth-shaking flocks
Upon the rippling grass- -where, small and pert,
The prairie dogs barked to the wind's refrains.
Our state, a place of everlasting change,
Where cattle now inhabit all the range!
Yet peace surrounds me as I drive about
That's not disturbed much by a farmer's shout
Nor "semi-'s" grind. Yes, peace and progress make
My state a healthy place to pass our days- -
And drouths and blizzards only sharpen wits!
We take pride in earning bread and cake- -
Employers round the nation give us praise.
We're literate, as Gallup's poll admits,
Since almost all of us can read and write!
We love our golden oatfields showered with light,
The glistening corn leaves, and the pasture hills.
We're proud to gaze upon our healthy youth- -
The independent boys and girls who learn
To get things done- -they're brown and strong and bright
At play, or work, or in their search for truth.
Of those who leave our state, how many yearn
To hear our meadowlarks and see the sight
Of vast uncluttered skies and plains again
And hear the jests of working western men!

HARVEY DUNN

Harvey Dunn is probably the most famous Dakota artist. He was born near Manchester, South Dakota and studied at South Dakota State University in Brookings, where a fine collection of his art is on permanent display at the Memorial Art Center on campus.

He also studied at the Art Institute of Chicago, and then lived in New Jersey as he developed his career. He served in World War I as an artist-correspondent. Much of his work from this expedition is at the Smithsonian Institute.

After the War, he began regular summer visits to his Dakota birthplace. These visits spurred his pioneer works, for which he is best known today. The most famous of these is "The Prairie is My Garden," completed in 1950. Said Dunn, "I find that I prefer painting pictures of early South Dakota life to any other kind, which would seem to point to the fact that my search for other horizons has led me around to my first. May I garble a very old saying: 'Where your heart is, there is your treasure also.' "

OSCAR HOWE

Oscar Howe, of the Yanktonai Dakota tribe, was born on the Crow Creek Reservation of South Dakota. His major art training was at the legendary studio of the Santa Fe Indian School.

He returned to South Dakota to teach at the Pierre Indian School and at the Pierre High School, at the same time sharpening his artistic talents. Eventually, he realized that what he had been taught at Santa Fe was not true "Indian style" but rather a substitute taught by well-meaning non-Indians. He studied traditional techniques that had been historically used by Sioux artists. He also was developing his own true personal style.

After his appointment as professor and artist-in-residence at the University of South Dakota in Vermillion, Howe was able to bring into focus all of the elements of Santa Fe style, Sioux Indian style, and his own personal style. The harmonic balance of these is evident in his most popular work.

BALLAD OF HARVEY DUNN
Audrae Visser
(Sing to the tune of Ol' MacDonald Had a Farm!)

Old Harvey Dunn was born out West,
A creature of the sod.
He ploughed the earth and mended fence
Where buffalo had trod.

Chorus: With a whistle here and a whistle there,
Here a whistle, there a whistle,
Everywhere a whistle- -
Harvey Dunn, he made his mark
A-painting prairie scenes!

Old Harvey Dunn was quite a man.
He painted pioneers!
He drew South Dakota scenes
For nearly seventy years!

At school he drew the blackboards full- -
Which made the teacher balk;
She scolded Harvey several times
And even hid the chalk!

Then to Chicago's Institute
He went for more technique;
Some other fellows scoffed at him,
But Harvey wasn't meek!

Two years in Delaware he studied
And then went on his own- -
Two hundred pounds, and six-feet-two,
A lot of flesh and bone!

When World War I arrived, they sent
Our Harvey Dunn to France,
And there he painted doughboys seen
In muddy khaki pants.

When he returned he taught his art
To youth in Tenafly
(That's in New Jersey) and twas there
The years began to fly.

Two men there were who scorned his work,
"A country hick," they said.
And jealously added too,
"He ought to farm instead!"

Well, sir, old Harvey painted on- -
The critics talked in vain;
He'd play his old harmonica
To ease the spirit's pain.

And now his paintings bring him fame- -
They hang from coast to coast;
The folks that used to laugh at him
Have since commenced to boast.

When he was sixty-eight Death called
And kissed him on the cheek;
And that's the tale of Harvey Dunn,
The man from Redstone Creek.

TO OSCAR HOWE

(Famous Indian Artist)

Audrae Visser

To you who knew the arid tawniness

Of western hills, absorbing in your heart

The clean austerity of prairie art,

Who, boylike, watched on hilltops, motionless,

While overhead the clouds began to coalesce

In sunset's fire, who saw the cliff birds dart

And lightning-legged antelope depart--

To you I bow, an ardent votaress.

For all this beauty that your brain has stored

Flows out your fingers- -orange, gold, and blue- -

Dynamic forms and vibrant tones on black!

The swift wild things that ran or soared

You capture now with brush their essence true- -

Somehow enhancing all- -and bring them back!

CHANGE OF FORM
Audrae Visser

when i was sixteen
my bosom was high and firm
and my back was flexible
all sapling straight
and in my middle
i dwindled
and then
undulating
my figure curved
out below to fashion
such cute provocative hips
that boys often whistled
oh what a body i owned

but through long years
i "tasted" as good cooks ought
ate leftovers rather than waste them
and my bosom grew ample like pillows of down
while my back swayed from the added weight
and before i was quite aware of a change
little by little my slim little middle
that beaux used to span so slyly
with just two hands, began to thicken
- -too many bridge parties and too many teas- -
the mints and chocolates, the nuts and chewy bars
were delicious and over-nutricious and copious snitches
broadened my rear. I consoled myself that friends looked worse
i said "i don't think julia has as good a shape as i have, dave"
and my husband with a twinkle in his blue eyes agreed saying
"indeed not christina you have so more MORE figure than she"
and for that crack i threw a cream pie in his face

Words to a Little Town That is Dying
Audrae Visser

You are expiring, little prairie town,
You who were once so bustling and so brave,
A home to merchant, doctor, judge- -and knave!
You never thought the years would drag you down.
Abandoned now, with buildings chipped and brown,
You dream of those who left with backward wave.
Is there a chance, before you meet your grave,
That you'll revive and grow, and gain renown?

No- -not unless you lie above some oil,
Or other wanted fuel. Just face your fate
In peace- -and rest now from the daily grind.
But not in vain were all your hopes and toil;
You helped to build a nation strong and great- -
What better monument to leave behind?

KEVIN LOCKE:
Dakota's Goodwill Ambassador

Cheryl Gorder

K evin Locke is a performer. He plays Lakota flute music; he dances the native hoop dance. But most of all, he is Dakota's goodwill ambassador to the world.

Kevin has performed all over the United States and in 30 countries on 6 continents (all but Antarctica). At festivals and native pow-wows, he is a major attraction. His name alone is known to be a big drawing card for any event. The reason lies not only in the quality of his music and his dance, but also in the fact that he educates- -and inspires- -his audience. His theme draws on the "oneness of spirit" of mankind.

His own inspiration obviously derives from his mother, Pat Locke, of Mobridge. An intelligent person, Pat is often seen devouring scholarly books, such as *Dammed Indians* by activist Michael Lawson of Aberdeen. (This recent works shows the encroachment of Indian lands by the Corps of Engineers for major dams in South Dakota.) An afternoon conversing with Pat will set anyone on an intellectual path, but surprisingly she is also very pragmatic. Her urging helps remind Kevin that being an artistic person need not mean that he forget the crucial business side of performing.

Kevin's performances usually begin with several selections of his Lakota/Dakota flute music. This hauntingly melodious music was primarily used for courting. In the insert that accompanies his cassette tapes, Kevin explains, "The Lakota/Dakota Love Song is a unique form, quite distinctive (melodically) from the rest of Lakota/Dakota music. They are dreamlike and were often intoned in the hush of the evening. The flute player would discreetly position himself so that, with the wind to his back, his serenade would penetrate directly to the heart of his beloved."

Featherstone, a professional recording company of Pipestone, Minnesota, recorded Kevin's flute music on two cassette tapes: Lakota Wiikijo Olowan, Volumes I and II. On the tape insert, Kevin credits the individuals who taught him the songs. Volume I includes the Lakota lyrics with English translations.

The education of his audience is an integral part of Kevin's performances. He patiently explains that all around the world, flute music originally was used as love songs. He obviously researched the subject thoroughly, and shows the thread of similarity that unites all cultures. This is just the first of many remarks in which he draws the conclusion that "we are all of the same tribe- -the tribe of man".

If time permits, Kevin will explain that he hopes to help people understand the art and culture of his native Lakota people. He quotes John F. Kennedy in saying that Indian people have been "the least understood and the most misunderstood" people in the United States. There has been "objectification" of Indian people. They are the only race of people used as mascots for major league teams: Atlanta Braves, Cleveland Indians, Washington Redskins, Florida State Seminoles.

Using Indians as mascots "depersonalizes Indians to the degree that people don't think of Indians as real, viable human beings...It removes Indians from a human category and equates them with animals," states Rayna Green, a Cherokee Indian and director of the Smithsonian Institute's American Indian program.

When this mascot image is used, it provokes all sorts of demeaning sports commentaries, such as one team "scalping" another. Recently, a CBS-TV sportscaster told his audience to "circle the wagons and keep the women and children out of sight. The [Washington] Redskins are on the warpath."

Indian stereotypes are also used to sell all sorts of products, such as Red Man chewing tobacco; Land-o-Lakes butter; Winnebago recreational vehicles; and Cherokee-brand clothing and shoes, to name just a few.

Fighting these stereotypes is part of Kevin Locke's ambition. He takes the time to explain that "squaw" is an insult to Indian woman. Most non-Indians do not realize this. He also notes that the name "Tonto" (the Lone Ranger's sidekick), means in Spanish "fool". Films and television have long been much to blame for stereotyping Indians.

INDIANS ARE THE ONLY RACE OF PEOPLE USED AS MASCOTS FOR MAJOR LEAGUE SPORTS TEAMS.

But Kevin realizes that his audience appreciates knowledge gained through humor, as he often interjects the lighter side of Indian life. He tells the story of one eager anthropologist who is spending his first summer on the reservation.

"What did you call this land before the white man came?" the anthropologist asks one old Indian.

The Indian turns slowly and looks at the anthropologist, then says, "Ours."

These photos show the progression of the performance by Kevin Locke. He begins by explanations of his dance. Then he starts with a few hoops and continues by adding more and more hoops, each movement showing a design from nature, such as sun, wind, and the audience's favorite, the eagle.

Photos: Cheryl Gorder

Kevin's performances spread goodwill for Dakotans in general and for the American Indian in specific. His special talent includes a knack for explaining his actions in a way that promotes good feelings about cultural differences. He ends his exhibition with a display of differently colored hoops that are intertwined. Then he explains that each color represents one of the races of man, and that each race needs the other races in order to survive on this planet.

Photo: Cheryl Gorder

The highlight of all of Kevin's performances is the hoop dance. Kevin carefully explains the purpose of the dance. "The hoop dance represents our philosophy of nature. Everything is a hoop. Where the earth meets the sky, the sky arcs over in a hoop. And the wind in its most powerful form is a whirlwind. Indians prefer to live in a circle. The seasons go one into another. And the particular phases of the moon at in a cycle. The whole world reawakens, comes to life. The hoop dance shows all this life."

Kevin starts dancing to the pounding beat of the drum. He starts with just a few hoops and winds them around his body as he dances. Each move serves a purpose to display an image. As he continues, he adds more and more rings. The images he projects through his hoop dance are sun, wind, flowers, grass, and the audience's favorite: the eagle.

His animation throughout the dance is picked up by the spectators. As he progresses through the dance, his intensity filters over to the audience. They can't help but get involved. There is a spirituality contained here, and it greatly moves the crowd. When he finishes, a ripple of continuity passes through the once-strangers-but-now-brothers audience.

The expression on Kevin's face as he finishes cannot be duplicated. He simply says, "Thank you" and the crowd is in an uproar. He calms them with a prayer which he says aloud and also in sign language. Sometimes, he uses an Indian version of the 23rd Psalm. Other times, he quotes from Red Cloud:

> *My Brothers and my Friends who are before me today: God Almighty had made us all, and He is here to here what I have to say to you today. The Great Spirit made us both. He gave us lands and He have you lands. You came here and we received you as brothers. When the Almighty made you, He made you all white and clothed you. When He made us He made us with red skins and poor. When you first came here we were very many and you*

were few. Now you are many and we are few. You do not know who appears before you to speak. He is a representative of the original American race, the first people of this continent. We are good, not bad. The reports which you get about us are all on one side. You hear of us only as murderers and thieves. We are not so....You have children. We, too, have children, and we wish to bring them up well. We ask you to help us do it...You belong in the East and I belong in the West, and I am glad I have come here and that we could understand one another.

Kevin ends his performance by walking over to the pile of hoops he has left standing. Several colors of hoops are intertwined: red, black, yellow, and white, representing the four races of humankind. The hoops form a structure that stands alone.

He explains that these hoops signify the brotherhood of man: all of the loops are necessary for the structure to stand. But if one is not there- -and he reaches over to take out a single hoop- - the form falls apart. "You need all the people," he states. "For without just one, the whole collapses."

Kevin Locke's entire performance has emphasized the brotherhood of man, the unity of spirit. Kevin Locke, who's Indian name is Tokaheya Inajin- -He Who Stands First-must have been named so by his grandmother because she realized that for Dakotans, Kevin Locke would be He Who Stands First as Dakota's goodwill ambassador.

People interested in contacting Kevin Locke for arranging for performances or for buying his flute audio cassette tapes, write:

Kevin Locke, PO Box 241, Mobridge, SD 57601. (605) 845-2690

or the South Dakota Arts Council, 108 West 11th, Sioux Falls, SD 57102. (605) 339-6646.

Norma Nordstrom Johnson

Although born in Bemidji, Minnesota, Norma Nordstrom Johnson has lived most of her life in Roberts and Marshall counties of South Dakota. She attended a country school, Norway #6, near Claire City and graduated from Sisseton High school and Northern State College in Aberdeen. She taught in one-room country schools in Roberts, Codington and Marshall counties and then in Sisseton.

As a freelance writer her articles have appeared in the books *Ehanna Wyoakapi, Marshall County History, Day County History,* and in the magazines *Dakota West, Good Old Days,* & *Lutheran Ambassador.* She has also written four TV scripts for the South Dakota Educational series, "South Dakota Adventures". Her weekly column "Wagon Wheels" has appeared in the Sisseton *Courier* since 1979 in the Britton *Journal* since 1978.

The five volumes of *Wagon Wheels* are Norma's collection of stories about the people, places, and events in northeastern South Dakota, and are an important contribution to the preservation of these memories for all Dakotans. A skit has been written and produced based on one of these stories. The skit, "Rose of the Prairie", has been presented numerous times throughout the Dakotas.

Norma's skills have earned her numerous awards. As a teacher, she has been selected to attend a special history seminar at the Lee Plantation in Virginia. As a writer and historian, she has been honored by the Dakota History Conference and has received the Annie B. Talent award.

Norma and her husband, Leonard, reside on a farm at Eden, South Dakota. She continues her welcome contributions to the preservation of Dakota history.

Excerpts from *Wagon Wheels*

The following five selections are from the historical collection *Wagon Wheels* by Norma Johnson. There are five volumes of stories about the people, places, and events of northeastern South Dakota. We appreciate her permission to reprint these selections. For copies of these books, write to Norma Johnson, Rt. 1, Box 62, Eden SD 57232.

WAGON WHEELS Introduction
Norma Johnson

If the wagon wheels of yesterday could have recorded their journeys, the pieces of our past would be complete. They left behind the trails marking routes to a better life. Also left behind were the numerous graves, abandoned shanties, ghost towns, old photos without names, broken keepsakes and yellowed papers proving ownership of land. These remnants of the past are parts of the puzzle of history. By putting these pieces together, we can catch a glimpse of that life. These are but a few of the stories I've gathered from this area. It is not intended to be a complete history; it is only the beginning of the search for the events in all men's lives, called history.

The church from the poem on the opposite page, as it looks today.   Photo: Courtesy of Norma Johnson.

MY HOME CHURCH

Violet Valnes Thuringer

Memories are such precious things
They can lift your heart and give it wings
To carry you backward through the years
To remember all that you hold dear!
Whenever I see my church
It gives me such a thrill;
Somehow we seem "closer to Heaven"
High upon this hill.
Pastor Gjerde confirmed me
The same day he died.
The Bible truths he taught us
Are still used as my guide.
His daughter, Ruth, was my teacher
For Vacation Bible School days.
I still have my report card
And it contained many "A's".
And I remember dear Mrs. Gjerde
(I sang Norwegian songs for her, too),
And also sweet "Grandma" Kluken,
And John—for the many kind deeds he's do.
I remember Marie at the organ,
And how well she could play.
We always gave her an offering
Every Christmas Day,
As we marched up and round the altar
And back again to our chairs;
The men all over on one side,
We would never sit in pairs!
The ladies on the west side,

I right beside my mother.
On the east, the men in clean overalls
Including my dad and brother.
I've attended churches large and small,
In places here and there;
But I've never seen an Altar
With which to compare.
The simple beauty of its truth
From Romans six, verse twenty-three
"The gift of God is eternal life"
Holds true for you and me.
How proud I was when I could join
The "Girls Mission Society";
The happy hours that we spent
Will always be a fond memory.
Klukens, Korsmos, Hoems, Stavicks,
Egholmen, Tollefson and Aastroms
To name but a few
Who belonged to our Mission Circle
And gave it all its due.
By learning the Bible lessons
And singing hymns galore,
And have fun at "gatherings"
We didn't need anything more!
And then our church was remodeled
It really did look neat
To see the green and white celotex
I though it couldn't be beat.
I remember all the fancy work,
The stand that had ice cream and pop to sell
At our annual Ladies Aid Auction Sale
That always turned out so well!
And all the Ladies Aid meetings

Were a family affair–
A social event for the family
Even the men and boys were there!
I remember the lutefisk supper at Engeviks
And all those good things to eat,
Those faithful aid members who worked so hard
Their energy couldn't be beat.
Oh, I was slowing growing up
And I went away to school.
During those years of World War II
Pastor Hyland preached the Golden Rule.
We sent our boys to the service
And prayed for them night and day;
We were also concerned for dear Judith
In a prison camp far, far away.
Pastor Hyland was the one who married us
And we moved to a different place;
But I can never forget the lessons learned here
That we are "saved by grace".
The faith and strength of our forefathers
Will always be a guide
To the members who still belong here
For their courage has been sorely tried
But they always came through much stronger
And they are so proud to say–
"Seventy-five years of progress
Happy Anniversary Day!"
To me it's a very great pleasure
To be able to be here today,
To see that my folks are still members
And many more friends 'long the way
I know how they trust their dear pastor
Who leads their membership few

But what they lack in numbers
Is made up by a faith so true.
A faith that has ever stayed with me
And helped me much through the years;
"My church, my church, my dear home church"
Through the laughter and the tears.
Forever may you stand atop this hill
A symbol to far and near
That here is preached the "Word of God"
And none need ever fear.
That it will change its teachings
That were preached to you and me;
The Bible is our only truth
And the "truth shall set you free."
Yes, memories are such precious things,
They can life your heart and give it wings!

Eddie Just, "The Human Machine Gun"

"**H**e fires ten shots a second with a .22 repeating rifle," reads the caption in a Believe It or Not by Ripley. This popular syndicated newspaper feature about Sisseton's Eddie Just appeared in leading newspapers in January 1935.

Eddie Just, son of Paul and Sarah Just of Enterprise Township in Roberts County, attained this fantastic feat as a result of hours of practice and determination.

His advent into the world of trick shooting was not luck but a natural way of life for a young man who loved guns and was fascinated by shooting.

There are also those who recall seeing him practice at an early age without any shells in his gun. Later he could boast of killing two gophers with one shot. Practice also included shooting at the empty tin cans thrown up in the air as well as hitting a row of tin cans placed atop fence posts. At the age of nine he shot three empty cartridges out of his Dad's hand.

A boyhood friend and companion of his, Oscar Krogstad, now of Browns Valley, recalls those days:

"We spent many years together, Eddie and I. We bought .22 shells for 8 cents a box in those days, 'course we had to buy 10,000 at a time which we did about four times. We were both pretty good with those .22 rifles. During the summer we would hit clay pigeons with a .22. Then we would hit the spent

.22 shells as we threw them up in the air. We hunted lots of prairie chickens and ducks in those days. We did some trapping, too," recalled 86-year-old Oscar.

Eddie was raised on a farm two miles east of the old town of Bossko. His sister, Thelma, recalls that Eddie spent hours and hours practicing shooting in the grove of trees on the farm. With his rifles he would often sketch faces on the tree trunks.

Part of his good reflexes have been attributed to the fact that he never drank nor smoked. Shooting the bowl of the pipe right out of his Dad's mouth attested to his shooting skill.

Playing baseball was also a part of his early day life. As a teenager he was a catcher on the Claire City Baseball Team. He also worked for awhile as a farmhand for Knute Walstad.

World War I came and he entered the Army and served as a Military Police. It was while in the Army that he contracted pneumonia and diphtheria.

Later he traveled with a carnival as a trick shooter throughout Wisconsin and Minnesota. An average-sized man, he appeared in western garb sometimes sporting a trim beard or goatee. His appearance was similar to those gunmen portrayed in the movies in the 40s. His secret goal was to play the part of a gunman in the movies, a goal he did not attain.

Another syndicated feature tells about Eddie keeping one-inch balls bouncing in the air, hitting each alternately with the right and left hand using a .22 automatic rifle.

In addition to his many guns he purchased a 1924 cobalt blue Lincoln automobile. This seven passenger, 4 door sedan, cost a little over $5,000 at that time (Model T's were selling for $400 then.)

Since the car was such a contrast to other vehicles it attracted a lot of attention. Eddie never learned how to drive so he had to have someone drive for him. As a result the car was used very little. It stood in a shed for many years until it was purchased by Samie Skjonsberg of Britton.

AT THE AGE OF NINE HE SHOT THREE EMPTY CARTRIDGES OUT OF HIS DAD'S HAND

Eddie's sister, Thelma Crim of California, tells about a special time in Eddie's life:

"In the fall of 1931 Eddie had booked concession stands at the Minnesota State Fair. Mother gave me permission to go with him. I had just graduated from high school that spring and I wanted to earn some spending money.

"We traveled in his old pickup. He carried camping equipment and all his paraphernalia. At night he rented a hotel room for me.

"He did not use his shooting skill but operated other games of skill. I sold the balls to the players who tried to hit the dodger. It rained a lot that fall and I wasn't very successful in the venture," commented Thelma.

Shooting did not occupy his whole life nor did it pay the bills. He traveled to Chicago, Illinois where he got a job with a railroad as a freight loader. He worked for this company for 40 years. Eddie died at the age of 80 years in a Breckenridge, Minnesota hospital.

SOUTH DAKOTA HOMESTEADER

Ella Lobben Valnes

Over the trackless prairie, he and
   his family came,
To this place so remote, to this
   home stead of theirs.
The land was rough and rocky—rocks
   make good foundations.
A stream of spring water ran sparkling
   near by.
Smooth patches of ground, he plowed
   for his fields,
A garden, too, he'd plant, for the
   soil was so fertile.
The cow could give milk for his
   family to drink,
And there would be cream and butter
   and cheese.
The hens would lay eggs to eat
   and to sell.
Wool from the sheep, would make
   Yarn for knitting
Caps and mittens, sweaters and stockings.
Long hours he worked, there was
   much to be done.
This clean new land that the
   Lord had created,
With all of its gifts, was his for
   the taking.
So day followed day with peace
   and contentment,
In this homestead, a haven, a home
   on the prairie.

THE IMPOSSIBLE DREAM

Mable E. Knudsen

Unlimited lands kept beckoning him
And teasing him, "Son, that's your way."
So he bade goodby to his home and his friends
And left his beloved Norway.

The dream he had dreamed had many a flaw
And doubts and fears overbore him.
But he learned to live one day at a time
And to keep his dream before him.

Many were good times with children and friends
And many times troubled with fears.
The thing that stood fast—the impossible dream—
Unfolded by bits through the years.

How could they endure the trouble and toil
With nothing to work with but hands?
How could they keep hoping to fulfill their dream
Of fertile and tillable lands?

"There's no way to go, but to go straight ahead,
There's no way to yield and turn back.
So we'll keep on going on day at a time—
Pray God to fulfill what we lack."

Now we still dream an impossible dream
In midst of industrial din,
With new kinds of trouble and new kinds of doubts
And new kinds of conquests to win.

We, too, must keep faith in one day at a time
And dwell on the joy, not the sorrow,
The impossible dream will unfold once again
And build us a bright new tomorrow.

LAND OF OPPORTUNITY

Dale Gorder

"**A**nd I had me this dream I was way up in some ungodly out-of-the-way place, in the middle of nowhere where the people are really some halfwits. Ya'know, kinda like those drips we watched that time on TV, remember? What was it? Oh, yeah. Waldon's or somethin' remember Jake? They had that drippy kid with the wart on his face. John-Boy and all them kids. Once in a while someone sharp would come through and just clean 'em out.

"Well, heck yes, I know they didn't have much to clean but lemme finish, will ya?

"Anyway, there I was and there was so many dumb ones, Jake, that I'd make a little off of this one and a little offa that one and when they'd start to smarten up I'd just go on to the next bunch.

"Shoot, take a cool dude from Joisey like me they probably would never smarten up anyway. 'Cause when Jimmy puts the closer on them, they stay sealed forever. And I'm gonna. You ain't gonna do crap, Jake. Thirty-five years old you was gonna be a hairdresser, and take all of them rich ladies money at $15 a whack for fixin' their hair. 'Fore that you was a jewelry dealer selling pastey junk on the street. Then you tried to tell everyone you found the Lord and to give you money to support your church."

"Listen, Jimmy, you and I aren't never gonna do any big scores, 'specially on those halfwits 2,000 miles or whatever yer dreamin' about cause they're smarter than you are cause they're there and you're here. That's gotta say somethin' about them, don't it?" Jake crawled out of the industrial dumpster he and Jimmy had just spent the night in and said. "I gonna make the rounds, you comin?"

Jimmy just laid back on the boxes and stared up at the early May sky and said, "Nope, I'm really goin' Jake."

"Aw, get real," Jake said, and walked off down the pavement.

Jimmy reached down and untied his Vietnam vintage jungle boots and felt inside. Out came his entire life savings: $360. He booted on out of the dumpster and kept practicing the name, "James Mason. Sounds kinda nice like an attorney or something. Respectable. No more Jimmy Kickey."

Walking into Grudge's store was a privilege today. He looked at Grudge, smiled and said, "I need the works: suit, shoes, tie, socks, hat and another set of cloths— some that kinda looks like Joe College, ya know? With the sweater hangin' down the back? And Grudge....I need an Iowa driver's license....How much is all this. And yeah, I want it to say James P. Mason and the pictures gotta be taken as soon as I get my haircut. Cut like the businessman next door. So how much?"

Grudge just looked up long enough to say, "Gimme a break, will ya? I ain't doin' no charity cases this week. My schedule is full. Now

112

hit the street Kickey."

"So lighten up, will ya? I said I'm payin', didn't I?"

A slimey smile spread over Grudge's lips as he said, "$300 bucks, cash. And sign a voucher for another $300 when you set foot in this town again."

"Who said I'm leaving?"

"You want this stuff or not? I'm a busy man."

"Ya, ya. I'll take it."

Dressed to the hill in his twenty dollar Taiwan suit, his fake Florsheim shoes, short hair, and a businessman smile, he had confidence. Grudge like the improvement so much he threw in a social security card and a Des Moines library card and a monogrammed tie—said JPM right there where everyone could see.

Getting to the bus station wasn't bad either. Some Yuppie picked him up in a BMW when Jimmy stuck his thumb out.

"Whew," Jimmy said, "I'm glad you stopped. A taxi driver trashed my bike when he ran over it. Almost got me to but I jumped clear in time. Yeah, I was just riding home from work. I try to stay fit by riding in the 12 miles at least three times a week."

His reply was, "Right. I ride to work as often as I can."

Hopping out of the car, Jimmy said, "Thanks a lot for the lift to the bus station. I'm sure my nephew will appreciate me not being late. He's coming in from Iowa, you know. Kinda a little green. He's never seen a big city. With all of those weirdos in the big depot, hard to tell what would of happened to him. Hey, give me one of your cards. I'd like to show my thanks. I'll call you this week. We'll do lunch, my treat! Thanks again, guy!"

Oh, Jimmy you rascal you. As he walked into the depot he felt on top of it all, carrying the dumb jerk's briefcase. He hadn't even noticed Jimmy getting out of the car with it, even though he hadn't had one when he got in. After all, every businessman in the Big Apple carries one, don't they?

First order of business, see what's inside. He sat on the bench to open the lid. What kind of garbage is this? Guys carrying around advertising brochures for Hillsville, South Dakota. Where's the good stuff businessmen are supposed to carry? Cash, credit cards, jewelry, naked pictures of their girl friends? He thought about dumping it in the trash, quick, as he walked up to buy his ticket, but he didn't.

"Where to?" asked the agent.

James P. Mason just politely smiled and said, "Hillsville, South Dakota, please."

JAMES P. MASON JUST POLITELY SMILED AND SAID, "HILLSVILLE, SOUTH DAKOTA, PLEASE."

Clyde Johnson had done everything right. He went to school and got good grades. He went to church and was an usher. He went into the military and after the war he had returned home to Hillsville where he worked as a hired hand for about ten years. Everyone knew him and he knew them. Seemed right when the job came up for grabs that he should run. So he did.

It was a landslide victory. Clyde Johnson—Hillsville County Sheriff. He was the law, the final decider, the authority over traffic accidents and a few bar fights, also capable of handling any major crime wave. Not that he was asking for trouble, mind you, but he could handle it.

Probably better than he could handle his 6-month-old marriage. Oh, Mary Ann was OK. It just seemed like she was like the rest of his life. Just fine. Everything was just fine.

He crawled into bed at 3:00 every week night and laid on the bed, thinking. Mary Ann was sleeping beside him and had been asleep for hours. Couldn't blame her. His watch was basically from 8:00 in the evening to 3:00 in the morning. During that time he drove up and down the streets or parked in front of the gas station on Main Street, just in case.

In case of what? Trouble. That's what they were paying him for—to handle the trouble. Most sheriffs were satisfied to do their office time and let the city police do the night shift and street work, but not Clyde. He put the city cop in the office and he met the responsibility head on. If it happened, he would be the first one there.

He had driven those streets on Saturday nights all through high school. He'd ride with a buddy up and down, up and down, waiting for something to happen—a new girl in town, a fight, anything. Nothing ever seemed to happen. As it turned out, the town never changed, only him. He just got older. And he was still there, waiting.

And now he was in bed with his sleeping wife, and there too, he would be waiting until he slept.

Morning in Hillsville was normal. Local businessmen were grouped around a few tables, having coffee and conversation. Delbert Olson the banker usually led the conversation. He didn't say much but he had an uncanny way of making the conversation go wherever he wanted it to. "Say Harvey," Delbert said, "how are we doin' on that little advertising thing?"

Harv said, "I laid it all out the way you guys told me you wanted it and sent it in to E. F. Holdridge just like we discussed. They said they'd get back with us, just give them some time."

"Well," Delbert said, "it's the first part of May and I've seen a few tourists already. Wish we had that stuff back 'cause it's about season time."

"Yup, know what you mean." Harvey finished his third cup of coffee just in time to notice the Greyhound pull up out front. Several people got off.

One particularly nice looking fella walked up with the driver, who said, "There's a fella here who'd like to talk to one of you boys."

The man with the fine looking three-piece suit, short hair, and briefcase smiled and confidently held out his hand to Delbert Olson and said, "Hello, I'm James Mason from the E. F. Holdridge Company. I believe you gentlemen have been waiting to hear from me."

"Well, speak of the devil," Harv said, and slapped him on the back. "We was just talking about you."

Jimmy briefly lost his confidence, but Delbert interrupted by grabbing his hand with a firm Midwest handshake. "Sit down, boy, have you had breakfast? Mildred, bring him over a menu and fix him up. It's on me."

116

James regained his smile and said, "Thank you very much. I'm afraid the food wasn't the best on the trip."

Carl Wagner, the local hardware store and sporting goods proprietor spoke up and said, "Boy, I didn't think when we got a hold of you guys they'd send a fella all the way out here!"

"Let me tell you. When the people at E. F. Holdridge take an interest in something, we act. And frankly, this town and your letter seemed to have piqued Mr. Holdridge's curiosity. He would have sent me by plane but he insisted I take the bus to get the feel for the country. Kind of know where I was getting, so to speak. And also he instructed me that there will be no charges for my services and expertise. Gentlemen, I am at your disposal!"

"Well," Delbert spoke up, "if that's the case, we can at least pick up your tab while you're in town." The dozen or two businessmen around pushed together tables. All quickly agreed. If there was anything all all they could do to help or if there was anything James needed, all he had to do was ask. And James assured them with a handshake and a smile that he would be around to see each and every one of them to discuss the town's tourist industry's problems and listen to any and all suggestions they had to help his company help them.

Delbert excused himself from the table to go get James a room at the Best Western. After all, he must be tired. Shortly, James found himself seated all alone in a small empty restaurant except for any overweight busy-body cooking for the noon meal and what looked like an oversexed young blonde girl in a short waitress uniform. When she had service his food, he had been busy minding business with his new acquaintances. But now they were gone and she was at his table pouring him a refill of coffee.

"Hope everything is OK," she said.

Jimmy leaned back in his chair, gave her his sexiest grin and said, "It sure looks like it from here!"

She blushed and said, "I can see you're not from here."

"Oh, how's that?"

"Well everyone else just looks and grins when my back is turned or else they make their little comments amongst themselves. It ain't often—no, I'll take that back. I *never* had a compliment on my looks. Save for my husband and I don't think he takes the time to look anymore."

Jimmy felt the friendliness and warmth of a woman from the country flow over him. He got all that just for one little compliment? He liked it, and he wanted more.

HE GOT ALL THAT JUST FOR ONE LITTLE COMPLIMENT. HE LIKED IT, AND HE WANTED MORE.

"Have you got time to talk?" he asked.

"As a matter of fact, I do," she said. "Might be nice to hear someone saying something more than, 'How about some more coffee, toots!' " She poured herself a cup and slid into the chair beside him.

It was hard for him to believe that someone so pretty could be so easy to get next to. He intended to press on.

"What brings you to Hillsville?" she said.

"A couple of things."

"Oh?"

"I represent a company in New York that is going to end your tourist problems here," he said.

"Oh? Gonna get rid of them?" she winked.

"No, gonna get more of them," he smiled.

"What was the other reason?" she asked, eyes wide.

"Well," he said, "that's a little more personal. I heard the word in New York City that the best looking little blonde in the USA was working in Hillsville in a restaurant."

"You ain't been in the West very long and you're already full of it," she said. Standing up, she took his empty plates and disappeared to the kitchen.

He threw down a $10 tip, half of all the money he had in the world, and before she rounded the corner, he said, "I don't believe I caught your name."

She turned, arms full of plates. "How do I find you?" he asked.

"Just ask for the sheriff's wife," she winked and disappeared.

"HOW DO I FIND YOU?" HE ASKED.
"JUST ASK FOR THE SHERIFF'S WIFE,"
SHE WINKED.

Out of the window, he saw the printer's shop, straight ahead. That would be his second stop. Into the grocery store he stepped. "Need some change," he smiled. He threw down his last $10.

Milton Coolidge, the grocery store proprietor grinned and said, "Sure thing, what you need?"

"Ten ones if you got 'em."

"OK," said Milt. "but you're not gonna need them in this town. By tonight the doors will be open to ya. And I'll be surprised if it takes the town that long to know who you are and what you're doing!"

"Oh," said Jimmy, slightly on the skittish side.

"Heck yes," said Milt. "Ain't many people come around to try and help a bunch of small towners like us for nothing. That boss of yours must be a dandy."

"You bet he is," said James, with a confident grin, "and I expect you'll be meeting him, too, Sir." He extended his hand.

"Really? Milton, Milton Coolidge's my name."

"Pleased to meet you, Milton. Yes, I fully expect Mr. Holdridge to fly out soon to help personally. He likes to get involved. So I'll be seeing you, Milt."

"Say, James, if there's anything at all I can do..."

"Don't worry, Milt, we'll be talking soon."

"Good—like to do my part, and sometimes more!"

"Alright, Milt, see ya later."

Printer was only four doors down. Not only easy, but close, thought Jimmy. He felt good because he wouldn't have to wear himself out to put the whammy on all of them. None of that crossing town all day affair stuff like in the city.

Jimmy stepped in and grinned at the first person he saw. "Harvey at the restaurant, right?"

"Right! If I can help in any way..."

"Well, Harvey, you can. I'm gonna need some business cards for my work here in the area—kinda let people know who I am and all."

"No problem. Have them for you tomorrow morning, OK?"

"Fine," smiled James. "Oh, I almost forgot. I don't have a phone number yet to put on the cards."

"No problem. We booked you in to the Best Western two blocks down for as long as you need it. I'll just call down and ask B.R., the owner, for your room number. Don't worry about anything."

"Great, Harvey. See ya tomorrow morning." Pulling out his fluffed wad of one dollar bills, he acted like he was going to peel some off. "Let me give you a deposit, Harvey."

"Get outa here! Your money's no good here, James. It's on me!"

"Well, thanks, Harvey. See ya tomorrow."

And now for the Big Guy. Across the street to the bank, where Delbert Olson would be waiting, hopefully with open arms. Mr. James Mason entered the bank, with a serious worried look this time. Walking to the teller counter, he said, "May I please speak to Mr. Olson."

She kept on adding on her machine and nodded towards a corner office with a large glass window. Delbert was on the phone, looking at him and smiling and waving him in. Somberly he entered as Delbert hung up the phone and motioned him to sit.

"Well," said Delbert, "I knew you big city businessmen are fast, but I never though you'd be working quite this hard. Thought you'd wait at least 'til tomorrow until we talked about the ad campaign."

"I'm sorry to say, Mr. Olson, that we may have to wait longer than that to talk."

"Oh?"

Jimmy nervously said, "You see, when I arrived the first thing I was to do was to call back and order number to have operating funds appropriated. It was to be wired to your bank for me to draw on. Upon calling, I found that the secretary is on death leave and the replacement secretary knows nothing about it. Coincidence finds Mr. Holdridge on a round-robin business trip to the Bahamas, Mexico City, and then on an unscheduled stop—which I have a feeling is here. I find myself unable to do anything but plan what I would like to do without the money. What makes matters worse is what is going to happen when he gets here and sees all I have is plans and nothing done."

"Say no more," Delbert said. "I believe we can handle this." He pulled out a drawer in his desk and found a promissory note. "Put your name here, James." he pointed to the line.

James signed, not really knowing what.

"Now, James, how much will you need?"

"$2,500 should be me by until I can get through to Holdridge," James said.

"I'll just need your driver's license," smiled Delbert.

Pulling out his new wallet and ID, Jimmy handed the license to Delbert.

"Iowa!" exclaimed Delbert.

"Yeah," said Jimmy, "that's why I was so nervous about doing well on this job. I only went to New York City six months ago and was lucky enough to go to work right away for Mr. Holdridge. Kinda my big break, you know."

"Well! You can't do anything on $2,500! Let's just make it $5,000!"

"Alright," Jimmy beamed. "Sounds fine, Mr. Olson. Real fine."

Walking on his way to the motel, he couldn't help but reaching inside his coat pocket to fell of the 20 little paper counter checks—the first checks he had ever had in his life. At least the first that had an account with money in it. $5,000—that's more money than any of his friends had. Heck, that was more money than all of his friends had put together. And Jake said these people were smart. As he walked up the drive to the motel, he couldn't help but notice the little late-model pickup truck parked in the drive. It said on the door "Hillsville Best Western". Stepping through the door, he thought, "I'm home!"

A short-legged little fat man jumped from behind the counter with his belly wiggling and his hand out. He blurted, "You, you, you must be, be, be, James Mason."

Smiling, James shook hands and nodded.

"Well, we we we been waitin'. Got your room fixed up, kitchenette and all. And don't worry, it's all taken care of. Along with whatever else you need. By the way, everyone calls me B. R." Still shaking Jimmy's hand, he continued, "Let, let, let me get your bag."

Noticing only a small paper bag with Jimmy's extra set of clothes, he said, "My, you are traveling light."

"Yes," said James. "Someone stole my luggage in the depot at Chicago. Strictly luck that I had one change of clothes in this bag with me at the time."

"Well, well, well, don't you worry, Mr. Mason. I'll fix it. You follow me." B. R. led James to the room on the end with the kitchenette, opened the door, and snapped on the light. He scooted over to the small refrigerator and opened it. It was packed full of every kind of cold food and drinks available in Hillsville.

"Mr., Mr., Milt Coolidge brought it over," he said. "He hoped you were hungry. Well, well, well, goodnight, Mr. Mason. If you need anything, be sure to call on the office. Or if your like, I can call on you in an hour."

"Thanks a lot, but I'm sure I'll be fine." The door closed and Jimmy pulled off his shirt, shoes and socks and looked around. He popped open a beer and said, "Here's to you, Hillsville!"

When he walked into the bathroom, he saw a flash of red. There on the shower door, tied to the handle, was a red rose. A note rolled around the stem said simply, "Glad to be of service to you. For more towels, etc., just ask for your Best Western Maid." signed Mary Ann.

Sleep came easily after he placed his 6 a.m. wake-up call. By 6:30 he was at the restaurant trying to make a good impression as a hard worker motivated to give everyone their money's worth! "Free breakfast and meals for you, Ace!" Mary Ann chimed with a wink.

Delbert wandered in as he was polishing off his breakfast. Delbert grinned, "Didn't expect to see you up so early, after your trip and all!"

Jimmy smiled and said, "Well, I guess I'm kinda excited about this job and you folks have been so friendly, I really wanna do a good job for you."

Before long, 98% of the 25 merchants in town were in the restaurant. Most were there for their regular morning coffee; others had heard that the man from Holdridge was in town and they were concerned with what the battle plan was. Before long, the cafe had turned into an informal meeting place. Jimmy stood in the middle with one foot on a chair like Mr. Authority.

"Well, gentlemen, I did some preliminary study of certain categories and it seems your needs fit into very generalized categories. It's basically the old advertising game. You break your money you have to spend into areas where its needed. Compare the money you're spending to a bucket of water. And you have six potted plants. Each of the potted plants needs a different amount of water. So you take your bucketful and ration it so all the plants get watered. Just consider my trained eyes in advertising as your gardener.

"The only real thing I need to know for sure, folks is, how big is our bucket? I've already told you that Holdridge is picking up the tab for my services and expenses, but that will still leave you with initial costs such as printing, billboards, magazines, layouts, radio, TV, etc. After you tell me what you're prepared to spend for the project, I'll be glad to draw up the proper graphs and expense charts to show you how it will break down—in other words, which plants need what amount of water."

Delbert spoke up. "James, we're way ahead of you. We had a meeting three weeks ago and we decided we'd all go $2,000 each. There's 25 of us, so that's $50,000, and then there's the $10,000 from interested parties who consider themselves non-commercial. And then there's the additional $15,000 that I threw in on my own. I believe in this town, James. And durn it, I want it to be the best place to grow in. I think we have a future here for the young folks!"

B. R. chimed in, "Th, th, that's $75,000. Can, can, can we do it for that?"

"COMPARE THE MONEY YOU'RE SPENDING TO A BUCKET OF WATER...FOLKS, HOW BIG IS THE BUCKET?"

"Well," Jimmy said. "I sketched out a preliminary budget, and I have to say we're gonna be close. At first, I came up with $100,000. Then I trimmed it to $85,000. If I work with cash and prepay each account, I can shave that $10,000 off the total. How long will it take before you folks can appropriate the funds?"

Delbert laughed, "How long will it take you to cross the street?"

Jimmy just blinked. Delbert said, "It's been in the bank for a week. You can draw on it as soon as I tell the gals behind the counter, which I'm gonna do right now." He pushed his chair back. "Excuse me fellas, got things to do."

"Me too," said B. R.

"Yeah," said several others and they disappeared about as quick as they had assembled, each to his own business matters. Jimmy found himself alone with an empty coffee cup and Mary Ann standing over him with the pot, beaming as she said, "Want some?"

Jimmy couldn't believe his luck at getting the job done so quickly in town. He knew he had all he could possibly get safely. He looked at Mary Ann, smiled and said, "Coffee yes, trouble no."

She filled his cup and turned with a pouty look to walk off when he touched her arm. "Mary Ann, do you know anyone that would have a real good pickup truck to sell?"

"Yeah," she said. "My husband, Clyde, has got a real good 4X4 with a small camper on it. He's been trying to sell it so he could buy himself a Corvette. But it seems no one's got the money to buy it from him. He'll be up about 4:00 this afternoon. If you're interested, stop over to the house and see him. It's the little red two-story just around the corner and straight ahead two blocks. You'll see the pickup outside." And she was gone to the kitchen.

Jimmy spent the next four hours standing at the pay phone on Main Street, jotting notes on papers, making calls, and looking important. When he had what he needed he was ready for the bank.

"Delbert," he said, "thing are moving nicely. After talking to everyone on the phone, they've all agreed to accept less for the jobs if we pay cash and if we prepay. So I'll be leaving in the morning for a few days to have the work done, and I'll have to take the money with me to prepay."

"Well," said Delbert, "I never figured you for that kind!"

Jimmy looked startled, ready to run.

"Settle down, boy," Delbert laughed. "I just meant you don't have to tell me—tell the gals over there what you want. Boy, you are a corker! Asking me if you can have the money! Ha! And Clyde asked me if you was trustable! Ha!" Delbert slapped him on the back and said, "If you want to get an early start, you better get the money now."

"WELL, I JUST NEVER FIGURED YOU FOR THAT KIND!...AND CLYDE ASKED ME IF YOU WAS TRUSTABLE!"

In a matter of seconds, Jimmy was walking towards Clyde's house with a bag full of cash. One block off Main Street, a blue Chevy 4X4 blocked his crossing the street.

"Test ride?" she asked.

Jimmy got in the passenger side and Mary Ann drove towards the edge of town. "How do you like it?" she asked.

"Looks pretty nice. So do you."

Thanks," and she kept on driving. "You can't go back."

"What do you mean?"

"Clyde called the Holdridge company and they said they never heard of you before. He talked to Holdridge himself who's flying in tomorrow. Clyde's driving around right now looking for you."

"OK, so pull over and jump out and I'll leave your pickup in the next town."

"Not a chance. I'm goin' along. I left a note on the kitchen table and told him I was going bowling with the girls tonight. He won't look for me until tomorrow and we can be a long way from here by then."

"Why me? What do you want from me?"

"Nothin'. I just wanna go. I'm sick to death of all work and no play. No fun, no excitement, no nothin'. Just the same old boring faces in the same old boring town. I got a full tank of gas and $1,000. All I need is a friend."

"OK. I just happen to be available," said Jimmy as he threw his tie out the window.

They blazed a trail across the Dakotas, Minnesota, and Wisconsin. Free gas, free beer, along with everything. He had the touch. He could get something out of everyone, just telling them a story. He was such a remarkable liar with a cute blonde that agreed to everything that people believed and remembered him.

It was a trail the Clyde from Hillsville County couldn't fall off of. On a Monday night in a Wisconsin campground, Clyde found Mr. James P. Mason, sitting by a fire by himself. Clyde quietly slipped a shell into the gun's chamber. He moved up behind Jimmy and put the gun to his head.

"OK, you piece of crap," he said. "I've been followin' you and some blonde for a couple of weeks and you're under arrest. The people back at Hillsville wanna know where their money is and I was kinda wonderin' where my pickup was. You dirt bag. You come outa some sewer. Drift into town, take advantage of everyone. What a scum bag. Scum like you should be stomped out. And that's what I got a notion to do. But first, where is the money?"

Jimmy said, "A man after my own heart. Put the money first!"

"Shut up, just get it! "

"OK! OK!" he said as the gun pushed into his ribs. He opened the pickup door and gave the sack of money to the sheriff. The sheriff looked into the bag. "It's all there. In fact, there's more in there now than when I left town."

"A MAN AFTER MY OWN HEART.
PUT THE MONEY FIRST!"

"Turn around. Put your hands up over your head. Move against the camper."

Jimmy did as he was told. He felt the gun barrel against the back of his head.

"I'm gonna make sure you never do this to people again."

"Wait! Don't you even want to know anything about the scum you're about to rid the world of?"

"I know all I need to know. You're a big scum and no one's around. I'm a law officer and you're gonna die trying to escape. A little excitement for a small town sheriff on a Monday night. Soon to be a hero while doing the world a favor."

"Did you know I'm from the Bronx?"

"Nope, don't matter."

"Did you know my mother was a prostitute? Did you know my father left us when I was 8 years old? Or that my 12-year-old sister died in bed with me from pneumonia in an abandoned building with no heat, electricity, or water? I was ten at the time and I never saw my mother again. I spent the rest of my life picking dumpsters to stay alive and running dollar and two dollar street scams just to stay alive. I finally decided I wanted something better in life, that I was a person and that I was worthwhile. That I could become someone. So I guess I just made it. Go ahead and shoot me. I don't care."

He heard a noise twenty feet behind him at the fire. Jimmy looked over his shoulder and saw the sheriff sitting by the fire and staring into it poking the coals with a stick.

"Heck," said the sheriff. "I was gonna shoot you."

"I deserve it."

"Maybe, but I think most of the reason was 'cause I was bored and lookin' for a cause to be important and you were it. Gun down the big city slicker outlaw and add excitement to my life."

Jimmy sat across from him at the fire, and Clyde kept talking. "I know it sounds funny to you, for someone like me to say he has problems, but I was never hungry or poor or cold, and I had lots of friends. I've just always been needing something that's never been there. I wanted to experience life. I wanted to struggle and win. I even wanted to lose, just so's I could feel it. I wanted a chance to breathe excitement and live it. Instead, I'm a paid public servant, waiting for something to happen that never does. I feel like I've failed at my own life. You were my big chance.

"I've even failed my wife. How can I face her. I left a note saying I was gonna nail you and things were gonna be better."

The door to the camper opened and Mary Ann poked her head out. "Did you get my note about the bowling?"

"I WANTED TO EXPERIENCE LIFE. I WANTED TO STRUGGLE AND WIN. I EVEN WANTED TO LOSE, JUST SO'S I COULD FEEL IT.

"What the blazes are you doing here?" asked Clyde. Then with realization, "You were the blonde!"

"I heard everything you said, and it's OK. It's OK! I only wanted the same things you did. I was tired of that small town—everything you said. Oh, honey, I only went 'cause I thought you'd never go with me. I never asked. I thought you'd look at me like a weak wife and I felt bad."

"And I didn't want you to throw it all away on my account," said Clyde. He pulled her from the pickup and threw his arms around her. They walked back to the fire by Jimmy.

Clyde laughed and said, "Well, looks like we got three big losers here, instead of just one!"

Jimmy grinned. "Not necessarily. Seem to me fate or luck or something brought us together so we could make some decisions in out lives."

Mary Ann scratched her head and Clyde asked, "What are you talking about?"

"It's easy. There's your truck, full of gas. There's your wife, ready to go. There's a bag full of money—a lot more than you'll need. Mary Ann did nothing but talk about how to add excitement to her life on the road. She knows everything now—how to add one excitin' thing after another. And with your law enforcement experience, you should be way ahead of the game."

Clyde and Mary Ann put their arms around each other's waists like two teenagers on a first date; wide-eyed and grinning. "So where does that leave you, James?"

"Real good," Jimmy said. "I'm going back to Hillsville and be the sheriff!"

They all laughed.

"Don't laugh," said Jimmy. "It's all I ever wanted. A nice room to sleep in, lots of good food, money easy to get, and respectability. Everyone respects a sheriff."

"How are you gonna talk them into letting you be sheriff?"

"I'm not sure yet," said Jimmy as he reached out and picked the badge off Clyde's pocket. He watched them jump into their pickup and drive away, both waving and grinning. He turned and started to walk towards the small Wisconsin town. He placed the badge in his pocket and then paused to put the sheriff's wristwatch on his wrist. Clyde didn't notice that Jimmy slipped it into his hand when he took the badge. "Well, heck, I just gave him back his wife, didn't I? It's 7:00. Still time to get into town and clean up for the night. Just a minor stop on the way back to Hillsville to be sheriff."

He didn't know what he was going to tell them about the money and all that, but that was going to be easy. After all, the law was on his side now.

Photo: Cheryl Gorder

JoAnne and Gordon Bird represent artistic achievement that combines traditional and contemporary styles.

Photo: JoAnne Bird

JoAnne Bird's bronzes are enormously popular. One style greatly in demand is the famous chiefs' busts.

A list of Featherstone's recording is on page 206. To purchase the tapes or to purchase art or bronzes by JoAnne Bird, contact Blue Bird Publishing at 1713 East Broadway #306, Tempe AZ 85282.

TWO RARE BIRDS

Cheryl Gorder

JoAnne and Gordon Bird are not just the typical talented artist/ musician couple. Their artistic achievements reflect the balance of old and new, traditional and contemporary in American Indian culture. They accurately depict their heritage in their art and music, and also bridge the gap between the past and the future of Indian culture. Their rare ability to balance the old and the new in their lives, their art, and their music is the reason that they are unique.

JoAnne Bird of South Dakota, formerly of Minnesota, American Indian, Santee Sioux heritage, produces art in various media—oil, watercolor, charcoal, pen and pencil, ink, airbrush, sculpture. Besides being in demand by private collectors all over the world, she has received several very important commissions including a bronze for the capitol rotunda of the state of Minnesota. She has received attention in all forms of media and is featured in *Who's Who in Women Artists, Who's Who in Minnesota,* and other national publications.

JoAnne's work has been influenced by personal interviews with tribal elders, subconscious and visual imagination and personal experience. She interprets her various themes in classic, realistic, expressionistic, surrealistic, mystic, impressionistic, cubistic, dadaistic and other abstract manners. She has produced sculptures in wood, soapstone, jade, turquoise and silver, pipestone, Sioux quartzite, paper and paper mache,

135

leather, hides, rawhides, sinew, furs and feathers, concrete, plaster, pottery, clay, textiles, aluminum, pewter and bronze.

Some of her most popular recent works have been bronze busts of famous American Indian chiefs. These are available through the St. Joseph Development Council of Chamberlain, South Dakota or by contacting Blue Bird Publishing (address in front pages of this book.) Also very popular are her contemporary alabaster sculptures, displaying a free form style uniquely her own.

Her work displays the generosity, nobility, universality, and humanity of the First People. JoAnne's work has been exhibited in Europe and in prestigious galleries in the United States. A list of some of her shows and exhibitions follows:

☆ *SHOWS:* Dallas, Denver, Boston, New York City, Chicago, Los Angeles, Seattle, Wisconsin Dells, Orlando, Atlanta, Albuquerque,and Phoenix.

☆ *GALLERIES:* Indian Image (Evansville, Indiana); American Art Directions (New York); The Indian Tree (Chicago); Kent Gallery (Sioux Falls); Floyd Johnson Gallery (Minneapolis); Byck Gallery (Louisville); Oklahoma Indian Art Gallery (Oklahoma City); JoAnne Bird's private gallery.

☆ *EXHIBITIONS:* Kramer Art Gallery (St. Paul); Pohlen Indian Cultural Center (Sisseton, SD); State Capitol Building (Pierre, SD);Mt. Rushmore National Monument (Keystone, SD); W. H. Over University Museum (Vermillion, SD); Brookings Art Festival

(Brookings, SD); Pipestone National Monument
(Pipestone, MN);Peony Ballroom (Omaha, NE);
Garnmeister Gallery (Sioux Falls, SD);American
Indian Art Show (Denver); Wabash Valley College
(Mount Carmel, Illinois); American Indian Art Show
(Houston); Squash Blossom Gallery (Chicago);
Karl May Festival (Bad Segeberg, Germany).

Gordon Bird of South Dakota, formerly of Minnesota, American Indian, Mandan-Hidatsa tribe, is making a major contribution to the
preservation of American Indian heritage by saving their crucial songs and
legends that otherwise would be lost forever. The combination of his
degree in business administration and his talent at producing, composing,
and performing has given him the ability to share with the world the balance
of the traditional and the contemporary in American Indian culture. His
recording company, Featherstone, has produced over 30 recordings of
historical and contemporary significance.

Gordon records historical songs on location at various pow-
wows and gatherings throughout the United States, with an emphasis on
Midwestern tribes. He uses state-of-the-art equipment for unmatched
quality. Gordon is not satisfied with second quality anything; everything
he does is polished to perfection. He can often be found spending hours and
hours working with his equipment mixing and re-mixing sounds until he
finds the ideal combinations.

Some of the recordings have been of Kevin Locke's flute
music. (Kevin is profiled elsewhere in this book.) Others are typical dance
music that can be heard at pow-wows. One interesting tape is a lesson tape

for the Sioux language. Since few people are yet fluent in this language, it's of supreme importance that this language be recorded for posterity. Gordon himself speaks the language fluently.

Besides the tribal recordings, Gordon has several contemporary tapes—good ol' rock-n-roll! His band, also called Featherstone, has been popular at Midwest events, such as proms and dances.

Gordon's business administration degree is apparent in the way he is capable of marketing the products he and JoAnne produce. Their art and music are in great demand because of the unique combination of their talents, plus their ability to get the right products to the right people.

Their talents have rubbed off on the rest of the family. Their three beautiful daughters: Jackie, Sherri, and Lori, are also very creative. Jackie is a promising artist. All three of them sing along with rock-'n-roll and traditional songs.

Dance is another one of the family's numerous talents. The girls have won many dance competitions in both traditional and fancy dance. Whenever one of the Bird girls enters a dance contest, the rest of the dancers know there's going to be heavy competition!

The combination of all of these talents was a factor in the Bird's family appearance at the Karl May Festival in Bad Segeberg, West Germany, this August. They were invited by the Festival's chairman to represent American Indians in song, dance, and art. The family, along with a new son-in-law and granddaughter, formed a complete dance team, with everyone except the baby dancing and singing.

The Bird family represents a fine balance of the old and the new in American Indian culture. They are able to use the traditional elements, along with their own unique contemporary styles. They truly display traits that bridge across continents!

POEM FOR WILLARD
Norma Wilson

I see Willard sitting and playing
steel guitar
in downtown Vermillion open air
or surrounded by his old-time, musical friends.
He loved to be with us.
He always wanted to be
where people sang and lived creatively.
He was never loud or brash,
but always had an even tone
gentle and true.
He wanted our light to shine.
And when it did, he told us:
"You have a good voice. You should sing more often."
He helped us keep old songs alive
"You are my Sunshine,"
"Will the Circle Be Unbroken"
"In the Sweet Bye and Bye."
And he left us beehives and bees
and rhubarb and guitar picks.
He left them at our houses.
This life showing us how to know
the great spirit within us.
We are all one we feel when we
love each other.
This was real to Willard
the only important thing.
The healthful good beyond material
comfort, what was good for the
spirit, what makes the people alive.
May he live in us.

Norma Wilson teaches at the English Department of the University of South Dakota. Her specializations are Native American Literature, Women Writers, and creative writing. She and her husband and their two children live on 40 acres northwest of Vermillion in a geo-solar house they built 5 years ago. Norma's personal writing shows and obvious conscience and commendable awareness of current issues.

In honor of Willard Lindstrom

WHY NOT SOUTH DAKOTA?

An exchange between proponents and opponents
of locating a nuclear waste dump in South Dakota
(Voices alternate from left to right stanzas)
Norma Wilson, 1984

Why not Edgemont?
We want to know.
Why not Edgemont?
So our city can grow.

The Atomic Drive-In
The Uranium Dairy Queen
Now a low-level dump
is the business we all need.

With foundations of uranium
our houses were built
But for the spread of radiation
we feel no guilt.

The Braffords have moved
and we're losing our hair,
but we majors of that city
have no fear.

Why not Edgemont?
The industry is safe
besides we'll all be dead
when our children have to pay.

Real growth is never sudden
It's never boom and bus
You want to welcome waste,
But you'd better think first.

You are used to radiation.
It doesn't bother you a bit
that uranium mill tailings
have increased our deficit.

You don't want to consider
your children's future health.
The only thing that matters
is your monetary wealth.

LIFE magazine
even featured your face
with a nugget of uranium
in your deadly grimace.

Consider Maxey Flats, Kentucky
and Sheffield, Illinois
and West Valley, New York.
Those dumps are closed today.

Why not Edgemont?
Let the Governor have his way.
If we join the Midwest Compact
he'd be head of the EPA.

Come on now, we need this stuff
for power, x-rays, bombs.
We need this radiation
to keep our nation strong.

Each season we will profit
from a million cubic feet
of radioactive garbage
when your initiative is beat.

Why not Edgemont?
Aren't you patriotic, hey?
Why not Edgemont?
Thirty truckloads a day.

If Chem-Nuclear builds a dump
we'll have jobs for 50 years.
That waste is low-level.
After that, who cares.

Fall River County
voted in June
to remain radioactive.
It's only democratic.

The problems we face
we can trace to thoughtless policy.
If we don't exert control
our lives will lose their quality.

Strength is what we need.
But strength is not in weapons.
Strength is in being self-reliant
and in harmony with the seasons.

You want to trade this million
for our seven?
Do you believe the promises
Chem-Nuclear has given?

Because Interstate 29
and Interstate 90 too
would carry those toxic wastes
to a dump at Igloo.

We do, for all we know
the fickle nuclear plan
Lethal for 300 years.
That's three times our life span.

And more so our initiative,
our vote, broader based
on us all, not just a segment
of the whole human race.

Let the good overcome the greed.
And let our values change.
And why not South Dakota
as the place for this exchange?

FOR THE TIYOSPAYE
Norma Wilson

We sit in the sitting room
of the nursing home for the
formal gathering—
Seth and Bob and Lisa and
Mary and Leroy and Imogene
and the Tiyospaye.
Calvin sings about
the 49.
Between him and Oscar Howe
on the wall is
a xeroxed calendar for
April with 19 days Xed out.

The Artist strokes the Eagle feather.
This softness living at the center
of life, strong and real.

A Brooklyn Mohawk fills
the university classroom
with the sibilant
moccasin .

A Dakota woman
reads her story
of Joseph Shields' son
the middle son
the finest rider anywhere around
whose bones

could not mingle
with the bones of his
grandfathers.

The heart beat of drums
and your wild voices
fill the building.
Forever the ritual closest
to this soil
this spring
and Hearing I can Feel It.
Only you can
keep this beat alive
this throb of life.

At the Wacipi
in the 4-H building
there is dancing
and Nancy Rock Boy sits
between joy and sadness.

As we walk over the spring earth
Grass leaves point upward
to light-filled sky
through the dry golden grass
of the season past.

Tiyospaye is the name of a student organization at Vermillion, the Tiyospaye Council. The
Council holds a yearly pow-wow (Wacipi). This pow-wow is now dedicated to the memory
of Joseph Rock Boy, a Yankton man who was for several years a Vermillion resident. He
became endearing for telling the history of Vermillion and the old stories. His wife, Nancy
Rock Boy, attends the Native American Awareness Week activities each year and she is a
source of knowledge, oral tradition, and strength for the community. In this poem, Oscar
Howe is mentioned (profiled in this book). The Dakota woman referred to in the poem is
writer Elizabeth Cook-Lynn. The Calvin mentioned is singer, songwriter, artist Calvin
Thunder Hawk.

Sioux Falls resident Adeline H. Lamb recently returned to South Dakota after 39 years in New York. She likes to paint as well as write, and often will write a poem to accompany a painting. On this page is an oil painting entitled "Sad Eyes" that accompanies this poem. The painting has appeared in the Sioux Falls Public Library in 1986 as part of a show.

PHOTO: A. H. LAMB

This is a closeup of the detail of the painting entitled "Sad Eyes" by Adeline H. Lamb that accompanies the poem on the facing page, "Sioux Falls City Limits". This impressionistic painting appeared on display at the Sioux Falls Public Library in 1986 as part of a show.

144

SIOUX FALLS CITY LIMITS

Adeline H. Lamb

Once there were no limits
Once it was all theirs
From the rolling prairie
That stretched as far as
The eye could see
To the Big Sioux River
That circles the city
And tumbles over
The great Sioux Falls
A glorious torrent
That has no limits.

Sad Sioux eyes
Reflect the pain
Of Attitudes that
Limit the Spirit
of Freedom
And Brotherhood
That once prevailed.

SOUTH DAKOTA'S SEASON

Carole J. Holien

Wind whisks across cold lake
Freezing eyebrows in surprise.
Algid arctic air at daybreak—
Icicles materialize.
Caucasic snowflaked landscape
Imprisons life beneath bleak cape.
Harsh hoar stillness reigns
Over captured countryside.
Barren bendy branches protest in vain
But wise elements deride,
Knowing the conqueror will be
Merciless frigidity.

Carole J. Holien, of Watertown, South
Dakota, often travels beyond the bor-
ders of the Dakotas, and she feels that
it always makes her more appreciative
of her own state. She is also a devoted
reader of South Dakota authors and
history. She plans to remain in South
Dakota but admits that there's a
"strong desire to move south for the
winter."

HOMELAND

Brent Lick

I. DEPARTURE

Linda dishes the last piece of pie

    for the day.

A smile for her tips.

    Just a table-setter.

A song on her lips.

    Maybe she can do better.

She heads to the lights with teary eyes.

    Like in the movies with silent good-byes.

Brent Lick is a 24-year-old teacher from Canton, SD and has been writing for about a year. This ballad-type poem has a unique style.

ONE PICTURE

I woke one cold morning.
She was packed without warning.
She turned and walked that day
    as the wind blew my heart away.
My world turned black as night.
I lost my only light.
I search for a place to stay
    as the stars laugh my heart away.
Some nights—I scream from sleep.
But that picture I'll always keep
Tonight—again my tears will stray
    as her face melts my heart away.

(SHE'S) ALL I NEED

(She's) a poet and painter;
    partly verse and mostly vision.
she doesn't mix for rhyme;
    doesn't wish for time.
She doesn't mix for hues;
    doesn't wish for blues.
I would regret the dawn and the dew.
Until I met a fawn and saw anew.
Her words are soft and sweet on my shoulder.
She is beauty and I am the beholder.
As she paints my world.

(She's) a poet and painter;
    partly verse and mostly vision.
Her clever prose is now easily traded.
Our forever rose has suddenly faded.
As she taints my world.

1st NOTE FROM LINDA

I was a slave of my energy
    and you were a master of doubt.
I was a prisoner of my youth
    and you were a guard from my dreams.
I was trapped but now I am free.
My treasure was buried and I hold the key.

II. ARRIVAL

Something in the city
    quickens my heart.
But for some
    it may become—
A stream of faces in an endless maze.

THE SAD CLOWN

To all, she is a clown.
To some, a night on the town.
She just wants to feel good.
Without some help she never could.
She will take anything to get high;
    do anything to make time fly.
Many say she has so much fun;
    more say she is on the run.
Whatever the case, we all see a clown.
She paints her face when she is feeling down.

BARSTOOLS

She came from there—
    heart was hungry.
He came from here—
    head was thirsty.
Eyes him through the smoke.
Spies her over the crowd.
She is trying to remember
    what he wants to forget.
Then, she will float with the words.
He will lies in the warmth.
Two directions tonight the same.
Tomorrow won't know her name.

2nd NOTE FROM LINDA (GOOD-BYE)

It was not thick
and was not my pick.
Blood has turned to rain.
The common portrayal
but final betrayal.
Blood has turned to rain.
Found calm in the dark
and comfort in the damp.
Now—rain has turned to blood.

A NEW MAP

Linda wanders out on shaky feet.
She meets an old man on the street.
He ways he was sorry
    and whispers his story;
They say there is a treasure
    and I know it is true.
It is deep inside of you.

I would always put in my time
    and call it my check.
I would always wait for a dime
    on the edge of a wreck.
I could always run that race
    and call it my life.
I would always keep that pace
    on the edge of a knife.
And, I could never pay the deed
    and sleep on the brass.
I could only smoke that weed
    and call it grass.
I could never call her mine
    or play the model.
I could only worship a line
    and jump in a bottle.

The man felt no one cards;
    felt peace when he shared.
Linda is crying warm tears to live.
We are here only to give.

SOME DREAMS FADE

Highway nears.
Meloncholy tears.
Old neighborhood jeers.
SOME DREAMS STAYED

III. DISCOVERY OF LINDA'S NOTES

MY LESSONS
CHORES

What is happening here?
What is happening there?
Feelings flow but so unclear.
Feelings go without a care.
We always seem let down.
Like rules had been set down.
You used years to build
and I will break the walls.
Because you have filled
softness deep in your halls.

OUR MAID

Sticks and cloth so clean and bright.
Every evening another glorious meal.
Answered every call, every night.
So much to learn and taught me to kneel.
Whatever I am or will be—
     my smile is her only need.
I am gone and blue as the sea—
     her approval is still my deed.
Thank you.

SNAPSHOT

No matter how we would act;
     it was love without tact.
No matter what we had said;
     it was nervous and misled.
In my heart I cannot fill.
     Emptiness I will always feel.
In my thoughts I cannot still.
     Innocence time must always steal.
There will never be another
     to match memories of my brother.

ANNIVERSARY

I found my love on a gray Sunday.
   He planted a seed in my heart.
      Watered by our tears
       and nurtured by our strength.
A rose, forever, in my soul.
And, the petals have opened
   to the same Sunday.
Seasons of this day move past.
But our rose will never die.

IV. HOMELAND

Linda dishes the only piece of pie
   for the day.
She gazes at the dusty street.
I tap my foot to a country beat.
Sweet apples and her hum fill our place.
"Home. I am home" is written on her face.

HOLY RELICS

Timothy Rensch

Out of the plains,
like the ruins of an
Italian cathedral whose cross-tower
is still intact,
rise the Black Hills.
Worshiped by Indians.
Raped by miners.
The cracked granite altars
are shaded by
living, climbing pine spires
and cleansed
by rushing
    flowing,
        rock-filtered,
           mountain blessed
           holy water

that reflects the
deep blue arch
of the high domed sky
and heals the wounds
left by man,
a monument to God;
holy relics.

Timothy Rensch is a Rapid City youth who is currently attending the University of South Dakota with majors in English and History. He has been writing poetry for just over a year, and he finds that his double major areas "spawn a greal deal of writing". He plans to write a book of poetry that would reflect the perceptions historical figures might have if they were brought back to life today. His poetry has been published in USD's newspaper.

THE FARMHOUSE THAT PAID THE
BILLS OF PROGRESS
Timothy Rensch

The Farmhouse stood
isolated
like a penny too worthless to pick up.
Fields around grew
tall and green.
Once worked and walked and loved
by three generations.
Now combed and pruned by
men in blue.
The gravel path to the section road
had long since turned to mud
and nurtured weeds
that filled ruts
of wagon wheels and rationed rubber.
Still
the house
stood
through peeling heat
and commando rains.
Someday
maybe
the company will tear it
down.

THE HANGING NAIL

Geraldine A. J. Sanford

Geraldine A. J. Sanford is a Sioux Falls resident who is an editorial assistant for *South Dakota Review*. She has taught at the University of South Dakota and the University of Minnesota at Morris, and presently offers courses through the Community College in Sioux Falls. Her work has been published in several small journals since 1983.

Gently she nudged at my joy with her nail,
pointing her finger at the old wives' tales.
Purring, I brushed all the nudges away
without any murmur of a scratch, tell well
insulated with fluttering promises
to listen to whispers others than theirs,
daringly choosing blankets and booties
and kimonos and sacques, before the fact,
each night sleeping with my hand on the pulse
of those burgeoning promises, my lips
shaping mute apologies to her Fate
for the audacity of my affront.

Over the years, one by one, all of the
promises were graciously kept, and yet
how dutifully I would test, with my
ambivalent hand, for the rise and fall
of each sleeping infant's chest, unbelieving,
waiting for my chastening, the stopped breath.

Even now, all of the promises grown
out of my reach, my hands flail for a pulse,
the rhythmical certainty of its touch,
guessing their breath, my own holding, waiting.
Mother, long gone, your nail is still hanging,
an odd momento, nudging and scratching.

THE MAN IN THE PICTURE

Steve Burger

Steve Burger is a staff writer for KELO-TV in Sioux Falls. He is a third generation South Dakotan whose grandparents homesteaded near Harrold. His story is about the Depression. He says, "While John Dillinger was grabbing the headlines, these people were slugging it out with Mother Nature, and their story deserves to be told."

"Grandma, who's that man in the picture?" The rain beat down steadily on the roof just over their heads as the girl and her grandmother looked through a trunk of momentos in the old woman's attic.

Grandma had struggled up the steep stairs to the dimly lit room at the urging of the girl who had been driving her parents crazy, chafing at the inactivity caused by the wet weather outside.

"Well, I don't know, Rachel," She took the picture and peered at it, adjusting her bifocals, and searched her memory, as faded now as the picture itself. A smile started then as she began to recall the occasion that prompted the photo nearly fifty years ago.

"Oh my yes. That was harvest time in...1936, I think. It was a better year than some we had back then. Well, let's see, there's Grandpa and your great-uncle Joe, and Clint, and..."

"But who's *that* man, grandma?" asked the girl, more

impatient now.

"Well, dear, I'm trying to think. He worked for Grandpa on the harvest that year but I don't remember his name. It'll come to me in a minute..."

1934. In Estherville, Iowa, as everywhere, it was the height of the Depression. Twelve years earlier, John Martin and his wife Emma had moved to the area from Illinois where they had both grown up.

Emma's dowry and John's savings were just enough for a small down payment on 120 acres south of Estherville, and they moved there to start their married life.

John had considerable carpentry skills, and his pride in the land, his work, and his new wife showed in the small, sturdy two story house he built for them.

They had no children. After two miscarriages and the death of an infant son, Emma had given up hope of a family, and turned instead to caring for her husband and the farm.

John was a hard worker and a good farmer, but the wind and drought were something he could not control, and one day the sheriff came and took everything, leaving John and his wife with calloused hands and broken dreams as the only rewards for twelve years of their lives.

The loss of the farm, which was the main focus of their lives, proved too much for Emma Martin. She left one day while John was out looking for work, and without a word moved back to her family's home in Illinois.

John managed to get some work here and there in Estherville and on surrounding farms, but not enough to get by on really. He began drinking heavily, and when word of that got out, there were no jobs at all for him.

Finally, in frustration and despair, on an April morning in 1936 he began to walk west out of Estherville and never looked back.

FINALLY IN FRUSTRATION AND DESPAIR, ON AN APRIL MORNING IN 1936, HE BEGAN TO WALK WEST OUT OF ESTHERVILLE AND NEVER LOOKED BACK.

John kept moving west that spring of '36, working wherever he could get a meal and a place to stay. He worked at a hardware store in Rock Rapids, and made deliveries for a grocer in LeMars. But being forced to work for someone else is hard for a man used to being his own boss, and always John became discontented and moved on.

The green of the coming summer that year brought no lightening of John Martin's spirit, for he viewed it through the barred windows of the Sioux Falls jail, having landed there for stealing a chicken to stave off his hunger. The judge's harsh words added insult to John's guilt over taking the bird in the first place, and left him at the lowest emotional point of his life.

In late June, he was staying at a hobo jungle on the east side of Sioux Falls when he heard that crops were good in central South Dakota, and thinking he might find work there, he began the now familiar trek westward.

He worked his way to Mitchell, then north to the melon fields in Forrestburg. He got on there with a farmer who never paid on time, and whose wife was as terrible cook. But, he was back working in the fields at least, and the sun and open air felt good after the Sioux Falls jail, so John was content enough to stay for the harvest.

One day during the melon harvest, he got into an argument with the farmer over his wages. A wave of the man's hands sent his ugly brute of a dog hurtling into John, clawing and biting, and left him with several bad bites before he managed to escape. He found a doctor to dress his wounds in exchange for a day's work. Then, penniless and sore, he moved on to Huron, then west to Miller.

So it was that John Martin was sitting alongside the Black and Yellow (the main east-west dirt highway in South Dakota), in mid-August, hoping for a ride to east his aching feet, while knowing the chances for that were slim. While he sat baking in the sun on that treeless prairie, he was stuffing paper in a half-dollar-sized hole in his left shoe.

Just when a growing thirst had convinced him to get up and move on, a truck loaded with second cut hay came rattling over the clay ruts towards John. A glance from the driver showed no sign of hope for a ride, but apparently he changed his mind for the truck came to a clattering halt just past where John sat.

John was up in an instant, and ambled over to the truck.

"Need a ride, do ya? I ain't goin' far, but you can rest your feet awhile, at least. Where you headed?"

"Uh, Pierre." John blurted out the only town he knew of in this direction. "Much obliged for the lift."

John could feel the farmer sizing him up as they bounced along in silence on the Black and Yellow.

"Need a job, do ya?" the farmer asked after a time.

"Mebbe...Uh, yeah, guess maybe I do," John replied, somewhat taken aback at the farmer's directness and his own good fortune.

"Well, if you're a hard worker, and don't drink, me and my brothers need a hand through harvest. It'll be seven dollars a week, and keep. You don't drink, do ya? I don't need no drunk workin' fer me."

"Never touch the stuff," John lied, thinking what the heck, I can stay dry for a month. He knew also in the back of his mind that the cold prairie winter was approaching, and it would be nice to have some money saved up.

"Good. We'll dump this load and go back to the house. We got a room fixed up in the barn, and you can start in the morning."

That was how John Martin came to work for George Hart near Harrold, South Dakota, during the wheat harvest of 1936.

The Harts had come to the area 25 years earlier much like John had, looking for a better life. They, along with George's two bachelor brothers, Joe and Clint, had homesteaded southwest of Harrold. Their life was hard, alternately baking in the summer and freezing in the winter. The previous years of wind and drought had left the once-fertile prairie barren. Years too, when the cattle had survived on Russian thistles and occasionally a few oats. But the brothers had stuck together and helped each other over the hard times so each could keep their land.

John liked the Harts, and one day followed another as the foursome of John, George, and his two brothers cut, bundled, and loaded the wheat and took it to the elevator in Harrold.

One afternoon late in the harvest, Mrs. Hart came out on the horse to bring the men some food so they could keep working until dark. She had brought along her new Kodak camera to take the crew's picture. When she brought it out, John jumped off the bundle wagon to get out of the way, but was promptly shooed back up by the novice photographer. "You too, John. You helped too."

The men all said "cheese" on cue, and the picture was snapped, but only one, since film was expensive.

A week later the harvest was finished, and John moved on.

THE MEN ALL SAID "CHEESE" ON CUE, AND THE PICTURE WAS SNAPPED....A WEEK LATER THE HARVEST WAS FINISHED AND JOHN MOVED ON.

John Martin was dreaming. He was walking down the road to his farm on a warm spring afternoon. As he turned into the drive to his house, Emma came out to meet him, spots of flour on her apron and her cheeks flushed from the hot kitchen. He looked out to the fields and saw a young man, tall and strong, getting the ground ready for planting. John Martin went to join his son and together they worked the fields in the warm spring sunshine.

The Hughes County sheriff was called out one day that winter to a miserable dugout hacked out of a hillside south of Blunt, in the shadow of Snake Butte. A young boy out hunting rabbits had found a man who had apparently been frozen to death for some time.

John Martin's body was wrapped in a canvas tarp and buried without a marker in a corner of the Blunt cemetery.

A YOUNG BOY OUT HUNTING RABBITS HAD FOUND A MAN WHO HAD APPARENTLY BEEN FROZEN TO DEATH FOR SOMETIME...JOHN MARTIN'S BODY WAS BURIED WITHOUT A MARKER IN A CORNER OF THE BLUNT CEMETERY.

"I'm sorry, dear, but I just can't remember that man's name," the old woman said after awhile. The girl was impatient by now to be outside since the rainshower had passed. "Grandpa or the others would have known but they're all gone now. I guess we should have written the names on the back. Well, maybe it'll come to me later, or else we'll never know who that man was."

I'M SORRY DEAR, BUT I JUST CAN'T REMEMBER THAT MAN'S NAME.

Photo: Cheryl Gorder
The changing seasons is
one of the reasons people
enjoy the Dakotas.

THE HIRED MAN

Alan M. Cvancara

Alan Cvancara of Grand Forks, North Dakota, is a university professor of geology, specializing in paleontology—the study of fossils. His writing includes several articles of a scientific nature, plus the book *A Field Manual for the Amateur Geologist,* published by Prentice-Hall. He also has a completed manuscript on ecology for the traveler. He intends to continue writing, but expresses an interest in doing some fiction instead of the technical work he has previously done. He also plans to further develop his abilities as a photographer. Future plans include a collaboration with his cousin on a poetry-photograph book portraying rural life in the Great Plains.

A colored man in the neighborhood? Paul couldn't believe it. He had never seen a colored person.

"Sure, he's been in the neighborhood nearly two months now," said his father as he pushed himself part way from the supper table and began nursing his coffee. "He's hired out to the Olsons, Swensons and Petersons so far. Others aren't going to hire any 'nigger' as they call him."

" 'Nigger' isn't a very nice word," his mother interjected. "And I don't want to hear you using it—is that clear?" She regarded him sternly.

"S–sure, Mom, I won't."

"They call him Sam," his

father continued. "Some say he eats a lot, others say he works a little slow. I've even heard he's dirty. But Pete Olson is satisfied with him, so I've decided to give him a try. Sam will be here toward the end of the week."

Paul could hardly restrain his excitement in anticipation of the colored man's arrival. But anxiety also tugged at him. Could he be trusted? Would he harm the family in any way? Oh, heck, what do those kids in school know anyway? But, then....several neighbors have complained about him....

When Paul returned home from school on Friday afternoon, his father was speaking to the new hired man in the front yard.

"Paul, this is Sam, our new hired man."

"How are you, boy. I'm pleased to meet you."

Paul accepted the huge, extended black hand, and nodded in acknowledgement. He was astonished by its gentle grip, not crushing as he anticipated. Transfixed by the man's face, Paul scrutinized the widely spaced nostrils, thick lips, kinky hair. White-flanked irises shone stark against the dark countenance but exuded friendliness in an unfamiliar way. The towering man stood straight, but unshaven, reflected considerable age. The whiskers, that's it! Imagine, white whiskers on a black face! Paul allowed his eyes to drift over the black body, clad in bib overalls, faded shirt, sweat-soiled cap.

Until then, total sensitivity to a nagging nasal awareness was diluted by his initial preoccupation with this man. Now, in the hot afternoon, he keenly sensed a body odor totally foreign to him. Not an odor of uncleanliness really, but like that of a strange animal. Perhaps the neighbors and classmates were right. Niggers—his mother didn't want him to use that word—no, colored persons were really different, odd.

On Sunday, Einar Gunderson and his family stopped by for a visit.

"Well, Frank," he asserted to Paul's father, "how much rain did you get last night?" A common practice in the neighborhood—particularly by the more pretentious folks—was belittling or downgrading of the rainfall received on their property. A vying for the dubious honor of "Receiver of the Least Rainfall" was engaged in actively. It was not that the awardee wished a showering of sympathy. No, more like a coup should he produce equally as well as his colleagues with the lesser precipitation, no doubt because of exceptional agricultural skill.

"Oh, about half an inch," Paul's father replied.

Einar glowed, "I got only three-eighths of an inch!" Satisfied of his victory, he pursued another subject.

"I hear you hired the nigger."

"If you mean Sam, that's right"

"That's one thing I wouldn't do. He's slow, eats a lot, dirty—like all of his kind. That's what the neighbors say."

"He's been here only a short time, but, so far, I have no complaints."

"There you go, sticking up for him already. But, then, only a Bohunk would hire him in the first place."

"BUT THEN, ONLY A BOHUNK WOULD HIRE HIM IN THE FIRST PLACE."

169

Paul's father returned Einar's smile, and impulsively parried the poignant remark,"Let's not forget that Norskies have hired him, too."

To Paul's farthest recollection, he had continually listened to the raillery exchanged by the many Norwegians in the community and the few Czech families as his. Friendly rivalry, to be sure, but Paul sensed that, at times, his father was not amused. Paul felt alienated at times, even embarrassed of his heritage. But trepidation over such embarrassment often led to sensations of guilt as well. He thought: Shame on you! Why are you ashamed of being a Czech?

The two families and Sam sat down to a special Czech dinner: potato dumplings, sauerkraut, pork roast. The Gundersons positioned themselves as far from Sam as possible, with Einar jockeying for the greatest distance. Paul's father loaded several hefty helpings on his plate, buried them in sauerkraut and pieces of pork, and poured pork grease over it all generously. Einar first winced at Paul's father's substantial, unctuous repast. His composure regained, Einar at the food offered him–minus the greasy topping.

"Hey, this Bohunk food is pretty good," Einar exclaimed. "But my missus will have to fix you lutefisk and lefse soon. Now, that's real food!"

"HEY, THIS BOHUNK FOOD IS PRETTY GOOD. BUT MY MISSUS WILL HAVE TO FIX YOU LUTEFISK AND LEFSE SOON. NOW THAT'S REAL FOOD!"

170

Paul's father shook his head so slightly that only Paul and his mother noticed. Paul knew his father was not enjoying his favorite meal as usual.

Paul saw little of Sam—after school and briefly during weekends. He grew fond of the man but had little understanding of him.

Then, school was out for the summer. This mean laziness and play for most of the city kids Paul's age, but for him it meant more, steady work. In effect, he became a second hired man.

"This summer I'm going to break up that eighty across the tracks. Tomorrow, you and Sam can begin digging and hauling rocks off that place. You can handle the small rocks and help Sam with the large ones."

Two hired men. Working together.

They used pick and crowbar to work loose the smaller rocks from the firm grip of the sod and crowbar with pipe added for leverage on the larger ones. Much of the time the soil had to be removed with shovels before the long crowbars could be applied. At times, a boulder could be only shifted from its resting place, sufficiently for wrapping a chain around it. Then, the tractor snaked it directly to a rock pile or onto a heavily-planked stoneboat for final transportation. The huge, completely unmanageable boulders were relieved peripherally of their soil entombment, and left for Paul's father. After tunneling a shaft under the steadfast boulder with a long-nosed spade, he would insert a dynamite charge and pour water into the hole for an airtight seal. In wet ground and with the appropriate charge, the resistive boulder might come squirting out several feet above the ground.

Although Sam worked slower than Paul's younger father, he

171

was steady, consistent. His respites with the cloth-covered glass water jar were notably brief. Likewise, post-lunch rest periods in the shade were shorter than Paul preferred. "Your folks have been good to me. I'll give your Pa an honest day's work," he would say upon arising from beneath the rock wagon.

Paul didn't mind the strenuous work and long days as much when with Sam. He was often complimentary, and concerned about Paul's well-being. "You're a good worker—and strong for a ten-year-old...Watch your back with those rocks. Lift by <u>bending those knees.</u> Otherwise, you'll have a bad back by the time you're twenty."

A camaraderie developed between them. But Paul still didn't really know the man. He could contain the unknowing no longer. One hot afternoon, as Sam raised the water jar to his thick lips, Paul asked, "Sam, why did you come to North Dakota?"

Astonished by the boy's unexpected question, Sam terminated the drink before it occurred. He thought for a moment. "Well, you know, boy, it's tough for a colored man to live in the South."

"Yeah, I can imagine. But even up here some folks haven't treated you very well. And they call you nig– Oh, I'm sor–"

"Nigger? Don't worry. I've been called that many times. But what hurts most is when it's to my face, and the white folks' eyes are glaring." Sam pondered Paul's question further. He wasn't being completely honest with the boy.

"I had a wife and boy. Both were lost to a flu epidemic. He was about your age at the time."

Saturday nights in town were special. A time for Paul to visit with his young neighborhood friends, go to a movie. But also a time when Sam invariably treated him to a soda or ice cream. Paul savored each treat-time with his friend, perched by the counter at the soda fountain. His savoring, though, was dulled by the incessant stares—no, glares—from passersby. He could almost feel them pricking the back of his neck, and wondered how Sam, outwardly, did not show that he noticed the glares.

"BUT WHAT HURTS MOST IS WHEN IT'S TO MY FACT, AND THE WHITE FOLKS' EYES ARE GLARING."

After their treat together, Sam would mysteriously disappear until the previously agreed-upon time for the family's return home. Not until near the end of the summer did Paul discover the explanation for Sam's weekly disappearance. One particularly warm Saturday night, Paul walked the streets alone as his usual young friends were unavailable. Unconsciously, he began searching for Sam. He passed several bars before something drew him to peer into one of them. There, through the hazy, steamy atmosphere, he vaguely perceived a tall man seated beside a table—alone. He clutched a bottle, staring dejectedly at it. It was Sam.

Through the summer, Paul and Sam worked together on other jobs; hoeing weeds between corn plants where the cultivator couldn't reach them, fixing fences, putting up hay. Finally, harvest time was upon them.

Shortly after the grain was shocked, Paul's father let Sam go as the work load tapered off. "Goodbye, son," said Sam, squeezing Paul's hand gently as at their first meeting. "But it won't be for long. I'll see you when the threshing crew comes through for your Pa's grain. Fred Thronson has hired me for the harvest."

Although realizing he would see his friend later in the fall, Paul became depressed and sulked for two days.

Returning from school one bright, warm afternoon, Paul gazed unbelievingly at all the activity: men pitching grain bundles into the hungry threshing machine as fast as the conveyor and chopping knives could assimilate them' hayracks racing back to the fields for always another load; grain haulers moving their precious cargo from machine to bin. Paul approached the dusty, roaring threshing machine, blowing straw and chaff onto a towering pile from a large pipe, augering grain into a truck from a small pipe. His father, the machine man, trained a watchful eye on the gargantuan contrivance.

"Where's Sam, Dad?" Paul shouted above the machine noise.

"Spike-pitching...to the south, I think." Paul wrenched loose a pitchfork jammed in the stubble, and ran off eagerly to find his friend. He knew that spike-pitchers, who roamed the fields and helped drivers pitch bundles onto their hayracks, worked harder than anyone else during threshing time. The drivers at least rested on their trips between the fields and the machine. Paul found Sam topping off a load; he sweated profusely in the afternoon sun.

"Why hello, son. I'm sure glad to see you. I can sure use the help of another spike-pitcher." Paul beamed proudly. He basked in the radiant feeling of Sam's treating him as another man. They began loading an empty hayrack. Paul skewered each bundle carefully so as not to slip off the encircling twine and scatter unmanageable stalks of grain. As the load grew, Paul struggled to loft the bundles above his head. Finally, exhausted, he stopped as Sam and the driver positioned the final bundled in place on the heavily ladened hayrack.

The stubble flicked at their dragging feet as they mad their way toward the final hayrack in the dim light. As they began loading, two drivers, abreast of each other, passed them by. Above the plodding horses' hooves and creaking hayracks, Paul distinctly heard one of them say: "Look how slow that nigger works. Fred isn't getting his money's worth out of him."

Sam straightened abruptly, paused ever so briefly. Then—he resumed pitching.

SAM STRAIGHTENED ABRUPTLY, PAUSED
EVER SO BRIEFLY, THEN RESUMED PITCHING.

That night at the supper table Sam was unusually silent, only picked at his food. He didn't even speak to Paul or his parents. Two of the younger men settled across the table from him. They wrinkled their noses as detecting a bad odor, stole glances at Sam, and chuckled sneeringly. Sam opened his nostrils wisely, glared back at them. At that moment, Einar

Gunderson, sensing Sam's irritation, blurted, "Hey, hired man, don't you like what the Bohunks eat? Maybe you'd rather have cornbread and black-eyed peas?" He guffawed heartily.

With that, Sam rose to his full height, regarded the smiling faces of all those white folks around him stonily, and stalked into the night. Paul attempted to follow, but his father quietly restrained him.

When Fred Thronson prepared to leave, he asked if anyone had seen his hired man. "Don't worry," replied Einar. "He probably walked home in a huff. It's only two miles across the fields."

The next morning, a clanking sound was heard as a bundle passed part way through the threshing machine. Then, the machine became silent. Paul's father tore into the machine's intestines, tossed out straw and chaff—and swore. A two-foot-long blackened cold chisel—apparently concealed within the bundle—had stopped everything. And, stopped everything for half a day, a serious delay in the midst of harvest season.

The neighborhood had pushed Sam too far. Most of the offenders realized this but were too obstinate to admit it. No one could prove that Sam had concealed the cold chisel in the damaging bundle, but who else had such a likely motive?

NO ONE COULD PROVE THAT SAM HAD CONCEALED THE COLD CHISEL IN THE DAMAGING BUNDLE, BUT WHO ELSE HAD SUCH A LIKELY MOTIVE?

Paul struggled with an approach to aid his friend, "Dad, don't you think some of the folks have been tough on Sam, making fun of him being a 'nigger', working slow and all that?"

"Yes, I suppose do," Paul's father replied thoughtfully, "but I'm upset with Sam breaking down the threshing machine."

Paul countered. "But you don't <u>know</u> it was Sam."

His father paused. "Well, no, I'm not <u>sure</u> of it."

Paul persisted, "How can I help Sam?"

His father pondered this question for some time. Finally, he said, "You might speak with Einar Gunderson. He's the most outspoken against Sam."

It rained, so Paul and his father visited the Gundersons the next day. "Einar, Paul would like to speak with you."

Einar looked surprised, "What in heaven's name for?"

Paul felt intimidated. He rarely spoke at length with nonfamilial grown-ups. But he mustered up the necessary courage, as at the time when he reluctantly asked his Dad for his much-desired pony.

"Mr Gunderson, I—I wonder..."

Einar regarded Paul impatiently. "Yes, yes, what is it, son?"

"D—Don't you think that you and some of the neighbors have been a little rough on Sam?" There, he finally blurted it out.

Einar seemed dumbfounded. "What do you mean?"

Paul continued, "Well, you know, calling him a 'nigger', saying he works slow and...and even that he smells bad. <u>Nobody</u> would like to be treated that way! He works <u>fast</u> for someone almost seventy— would you work as fast if you was almost seventy? How can you..." Paul began to sob, and couldn't believe what he had just said to Mr. Gunderson.

Such an outburst from a young lad was totally foreign to Einar. But he appreciated the boy's sincerity, and was moved by his torment.

"Son," he reluctantly admitted what he was about to say, "you might be right about some of this. I'll think about our, ah, discussion, and maybe mention it to a few neighbors." Einar didn't wish to overly commit himself.

After the fields dried and skies cleared, the threshing crew shifted to Einar's place. On Saturday, Paul's father allowed his son to help out at Einar's. As Sam and Paul spike-pitched, they both received friendly smiles and easy conversation.

That night, at supper, everyone ate jovially. As the pie was served, Einar rose from the table, clearing his throat.

"Neighbors," he paused, this being difficult for him. "I—I'd like you to recognize a couple of good workers—Sam and Paul. Sam, you'll be heading home in a few days...maybe you can use a new dress shirt." And, almost in the same motion as he presented Sam the gift, Einar stuffed two dollars in Paul's shirt pocket.

The hired men, seated together, beamed proudly, contentedly.

"I'D LIKE YOU TO RECOGNIZE A COUPLE OF GOOD WORKERS—SAM AND PAUL...."
THE HIRED MEN, SEATED TOGETHER,
BEAMED PROUDLY, CONTENTEDLY.

THE SPIRIT OF THE PIONEER

Rachel Walradth

Rachel Waldrath was editor of the *White Leader,* of White, South Dakota, for many years. She had a strong devotion to the White community and a strong interest in history. In 1967, at the age of 89, Rachel was still hard at work as the editor and publisher of the paper. People fondly remember her as a keystone member of the community.

The settler in Dakota
Took an honest pride
In turning a long straight furrow
Across his acres wide.
As he cut the shining furrow
He dreamed of future days
When he hoped his sons and daughters
Might tread in better ways.
The bigness of the landscape
Became a part of his soul,
As he gazed at the far horizon
Or at his furrow's goal.
The upturned sod's clean odor
Gave promise of golden grain;
He felt through rain and sunshine
His labor was not in vain.
With faith as wide as the prairie,
And hope as high as the sky,
He broke his good straight furrow—
And so should you and I.

SPECIAL
JUVENILE
SECTION

SILENCE

Jennifer Johnson

Silence is the morning sky,
Silence is the desert dry,

Silence is a bird alone
Silence is a quiet tone.

Jennifer Johnson, now 16, wrote this poem when she was 11. She still enjoys writing because it helps her express her feelings. Jennifer is a resident of Sioux Falls, SD. Her grandmother, Bertha O. Johnson, submitted this poem.

TRUE PERSPECTIVE

Erin Jansa

I stood alone in the Midwestern
empty field, letting the dark fold
in around me like a blanket. The
cold winter night air seemed not to
notice my presence, and pulled at
my warm goose down jacket. The starched
brown lifeless grass spiked from
December's frosted ground; no snow
studded this December scene. The
velvet black sky had cold white
sequins sewn to its body—and the
moon illuminated my stone face as
I inhaled the crisp smell of winter
and squinted into the everlasting
horizon at the glow of the city lights.
I stood in the field like a cornstalk
and outstretched my arms—not even
coming close to encompassing the
broadness, and in my mind I could
almost fathom the size of the Earth

Erin Jansa, 17, of Sioux Falls, SD,
writes for personal satisfaction, but
also dreams of developing a career that
includes writing. She hopes to travel
the US after graduating from college
and then write about her experiences.

SCARECROW

Erin Jansa

The tall crispy husks whispered softly as they swayed in the October wind. The golden shells of summer's harvest sang to each other in husky, deep voices of a blues singer. The vibrating sun above coated the earth in rays of soothing warm light. He stood in the midst of the dancing stalks, alone, like a tourist in another country. His breath never permeated the crisp air, his eyes never wandered from the far-off horizon of blazing sunlight. His arms never twitched. He stood in the midst of the corn skeletons; he listened to their incessant raspy voices as they told their secrets of the coming season. He let himself be host to the fluttering black pests of his flock of whisperers; they could stay now; he had nothing left to protect. He stood immobile awaiting the approach of the killer frost when he could close his eyes and abandon his summer job.

SOUTH DAKOTA: 1986

Wendy Jane Larson

In the winter there it is, an ice block
And in the summer, a nice, warm lake.
And in the spring, the fields are being planted
And in autumn, the crops get harvested.

Only in this great place
Can every tribe and race
Have the variety Dakota brings
To everyone and everything.

So many days I long to hear
"South Dakota did better this year
Better in its worthy ways",
That'll happen, one of these days.

Wendy Jane Larson of Langford, South Dakota, 15, has written essays, poems, and stories for numerous local organizations. Senator Tom Daschle has a personal scrapbook of her work that she has sent him. In college, she plans to major in mass communications–broadcasting. She wants to become a reporter and an anchor on a major network news team. One of her long-term goals is to write and publish a novel.

COUNTRY'S BEAUTY

Wendy Jane Larson

Looking out into the sky
I see beautiful things.
In the daytime, the birds fly,
And at night, stars grace the sky.

The trees have something to show.
The beautiful fall leaves
And the animals, we know,
Who live their lives in the tree and its holes.

The small things we see each day
Are often taken for granted.
But all are beautiful in a special way.
If we just take the time to look each day.

WHY SPIRIT MOUND IS SPECIAL

Lynn Monfore

Lynn Monfore, 12, of Vermillion, South Dakota, likes creative writing for fun. She wants to be a pilot and an astronaut for NASA. Her father has a two-person Cessna, and Lynn is anxious to fly it! She has a large collection of stuffed animals—114 in all, and hopes to hit 200 soon. We would like to thank her teacher, Betsy Noll, of Vermillion Middle School for submitting Lynn's work.

In 1804, Meriwether Lewis and William Clark were sent by Thomas Jefferson to explored the Louisiana Purchase. After two months, Lewis and Clark got to South Dakota. Below the bluff of Vermillion, South Dakota, by the Vermillion River, they stopped and made camp for the night. In the morning, they climbed up the bluff and continued north until they got to another bend in the Vermillion River. From there, they crossed and went up a small mound made of Niobrara Marl. They had heard about the mound from the Indians. The Indians believed that little devils and spirits roamed on the mound. That is how the name Spirit Mound came about. From the top of Spirit Mound, Lewis and Clark described in their journal that they could see buffalo in all directions and only two or three trees.

Now, today, there stands a feed lot on Spirit Mound, eroding away part of South Dakota's history. It is owned privately so people can't do much about it; however a group of people who care about history are trying to preserve Spirit Mound and turn it into a park so that people now, or in the future, can go and see what Lewis and Clark saw when they were here in South Dakota so very long ago in 1804.

Spirit Mound may only be a mound of dirt, but Spirit Mound is special because it is one of the few locations that could be identified and found today.

If you are interested in helping preserve Spirit Mound, or are interested in knowing more about Spirit Mound, write to:

Lewis & Clark Spirit Mound Trust, Inc.
South Dakota Historical Preservation Office
PO Box 417
Vermillion, SD 57069

THIS IS HOW SPIRIT MOUND LOOKS TODAY

Sarah Gorder, 13, born in South Dakota, enjoys sketching and writing, especially about native American subjects. She has had her poetry published in *Children's Digest*. She collects antique Indian dolls.

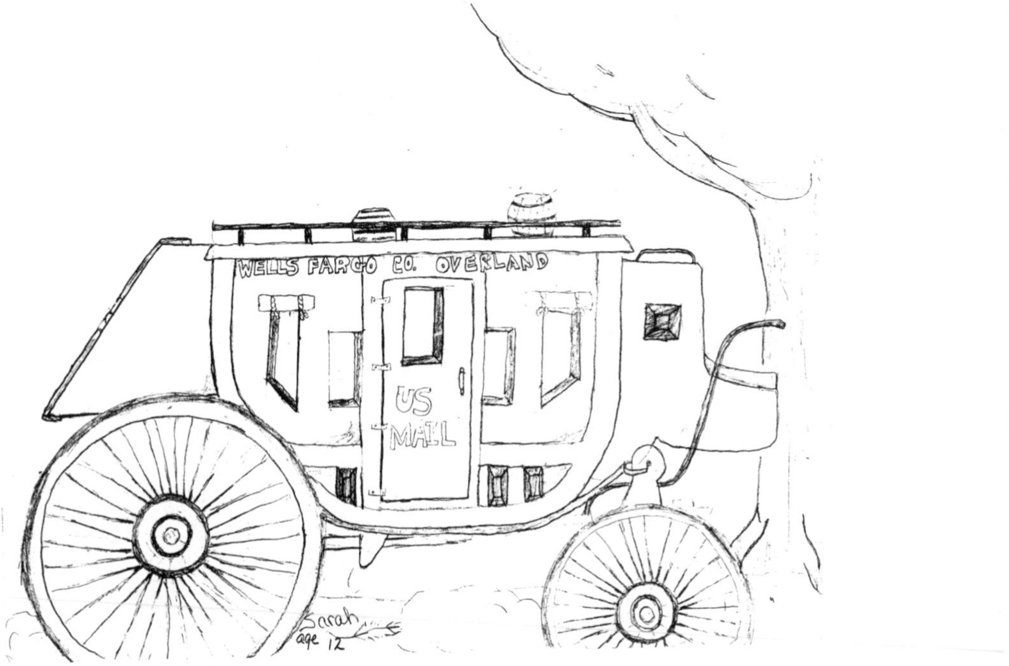
WELLS FARGO CO. OVERLAND
US
MAIL
Sarah
age 12

Stagecoach Sketch by Sarah Gorder

THE REAL WORLD
Maria del Carmen Perez

On days like this when skies seem grey
Even though the sun shines more brightly than ever
When the weatherman declares today
As the warmest this winter
Nonetheless, I shiver
Because of a paralyzing chill in my heart

I usually envision a brand new tomorrow
God should make things better
The balance of nature clearly indicates
That we must all have bad days to earn good ones.
But everyday becomes worse
I sink further and deeper in a quicksand
Of disappointment, depression, and much deception
At home, in school, everywhere
I realize that there is no Tarzan out there

My childhood innocence and ideals shattered
My spirit and soul battered
By this cruel, impossible, perfectionistic world
Nothing look good, anymore
Tears have blinded my once searching eyes

War at home
War in school
War all over the world
Where lies the peace?....

What is peace?

Maria del Carmen Perez,16, of Fargo, North
Dakota, is a   co-editor of her high school
newspaper, *Shack.* Her goal is to become an
accomplished journalist. She praises her teachers Suzanne Foster, Mark Joraanstad, and Mary
Wright, for helping her develop communication
skills. She says, "I'm glad they were there."

REUNION

Maria del Carmen Perez

My first day in college at U. C. Berkeley was hot and humid, but once in awhile, a cool breeze from the ocean penetrated the warm air. Uncomfortable in the sweltering heat, I squirmed in my seat. I casually looked around and noticed an oddly familiar boy in the next seat. Sweat trickled from his brow, and he wiped the drop of moisture with the back of his hand.

"Oooh!" he groaned, licking his dry, chapped lips. "With this California weather, I might die from a heat stroke." He smiled and revealed a set of blindingly dazzling, white teeth.

Smiling my you're-my-number-one smile, I replied, "Don't worry, you won't die. I'm a certified Red Cross first-aider." My eyes studied his face meticulously and noticed a resemblance to someone I knew back home in North Dakota. But he couldn't be! He looked just like the identical twin of Ron Davies, my first real crush. After all these years, he suddenly reappeared in my life! These things only happened on television or romance novels, for heaven's sakes. No, that boy was not him. I shook my head, no.

I ventured to ask, "You said, 'California weather'. Aren't you from here?"

"No, I'm from—" he did not have time to finish. Up front of the room, the professor commanded everyone's attention.

"Everyone! Please behave yourselves," he shouted in a rather pompous Alfred Hitchcock voice. "May I remind you that you are no longer in high school. However, for most, this is your first day. Therefore, I shall forgive your unnecessary chatter." Alfred went on to explain his rules and regulations.

After the interminable and quite boring lecture, he announced, "I believe that it is important for us to acquaint ourselves with one another. This act enables us to discuss more openly and freely in class. Indeed, sharing opinions with friends is easier than among strangers." He paused to take a breath. "I want each person to stand up, tell us his name and amuse us with an anecdote about himself—or herself. Now, let's start with you."

He pointed to the familiar boy next to me.

With faint traces of embarrassment highlighting his cheeks, he said, "I'm Ron Davies and I—uh, come from North Dakota."

I gasped. No, it can't be. Not Ron! Quickly, I composed myself and tried not to show any signs of recognition. I remembered the past.

Ron, yes Ron, was the first victim of my adolescent affections. Like many teenagers of this age, I did a lot of embarrassing things, many of which are too painful to recall. I liked him very much, and a few said that yes, he liked me too. However, some said that he hated my guts and thought I was 'an old bag'. Everyone teased us and called out each time we were in the same room, "Hey Ron, there's Chick" (my nickname in high school My real name is Regina Maria del Carmen Christina Arambulo Perez. Rather long, isn't it?) Nonetheless, wanting to express myself, I stupidly sent him a singing telegram without reading its contents first. Of course, I should have "looked before leaping". I jumped in my seat when I first heard the words sung to the tune of "You Are My Sunshine": *"You are my sweetheart, my only sweetheart. You make me happy..."* Being oriental, it was a good thing that I never blushed.

Many girls thought him to be overly conceited; this soon led to his unpopularity. He left in the middle of his junior year and transferred to a different school. One girl commented, "He was no longer Mr. Cool. That's why he moved. His system could not take it!"

"Excuse me, madame," the professor called out crossly. Ron nudged me, waking me from my thoughts. "I do believe that it is your turn."

"Oh," I uttered, not quite knowing what to say next. "My name is, um," I sneaked a sideways look at Ron and wished that he suddenly became deaf for a moment or that the floor underneath me suddenly gave way. I just did not want him to know who I really was. I wonder if it was too late to explain to Alfred Hitchcock that I 'may' have been in the wrong class and then run to the office and change my schedule. Maybe, if I suddenly fainted, they would have to rush me to the hospital and I would change my schedule there.

"Is something wrong?" the professor bellowed. "Did you forget your real name?"

I have the professor a you're-number-one smile. "My name is rather long. You know us foreigners—um—uh—we like long names that are really hard to pronounce. Um, I guess it protects us from the government! You know, dictators who want to have you killed. So, why don't you just call me...Crissy?"

Ron leaned over and whispered, "What happened to 'Chick'?"

"WHAT HAPPENED TO 'CHICK'?"

SOUTH DAKOTA

Mary Ann Hofer

We appreciate the many teachers who submitted work from their students for this book. To show our appreciation, we would like to profile one of these teachers, Mary Ann Hofer of the Elementary Unique Learning Experiences program in Sioux Falls, South Dakota.

The program is designed to help students become more independent and to aid in their development of personal growth and their specific strengths and talents. Gifted students are encouraged to challenge each other through a flexible format that allows them to recognize their own needs and abilities. This program provides new and challenging learning experiences that are not ordinarily included in regular classroom curriculum. At the elementary level, there are 9 staff members who serve students in 21 schools in Sioux Falls.

Mary Ann Hofer enjoys her work with the ULE program. Besides teaching, she in involved with musical groups, both instrumental and vocal, such as the Sweet Adelines. With her busy schedule, she says that, "Writing is a dream yet to be fulfilled."

Sunshine State
Oglala Sioux Indian Reservation
Under God the People Rule
Tom Brokaw
Huron State Fair

Dakota Badlands & Black Hills
American pasqueflower
KELO-land radio and TV
Oscar Howe
Tom & Curt Byrum
Augustana College

South Dakota is truly a land of infinite variety.

MOUNT RUSHMORE

Angela Kiefer

Made of granite
Gray-colored stone,
It's in South Dakota
And that's our home.

There's Washington, Lincoln,
Roosevelt and Jefferson too.
Faces carved in stone
And you ask, designed by whom?

It's Gutzon Borglum
That's his name,
It took fourteen years
But to us it's all the same.

National Monument,
Expression of time,
Beauty beyond words,
A sight to behold.

Angela Kiefer, 12, of Sioux Falls is a student of Mary Ann Hofer in the ULE program. She's had poetry published in *Prairie Winds*, a South Dakota magazine. She would like to be a doctor, but for now she enjoys writing just for fun.

Harmony Schuttler, 12, of Sioux Falls, a student of Mary Ann Hofer, enjoys drawing pictures of unicorns, animals, and people. She also draws pictures to go along with her stories. She has written various plays which were presented by members of her class. She plans to continue to keep art a part of her life.

Joshua Johnson, 12, of Sioux Falls, a student of Mary Ann Hofer, is a native South Dakotan. He would like to be a fireman or a veterinarian. For now, his hobbies are art, sticker collecting, and gymnastics.

199

SOUTH DAKOTA

Cece White

I say I'm from South Dakota,
"South Dakota," a New Yorker asks,
As if I'm from Transylvania or
Someplace from the past.

They just don't know about our state,
It's beauty, bounty, and life.

No, it's not flashy, blase or unique,
It's down to earth and sort of plain.

But plainness has its wonders, and we,
As South Dakotans believe that our land
Is a wonder by itself.

Cece White, 12, of Sioux Falls, a student of Mary Ann Hofer, has been to six foreign countries. She has had poetry published in *Prism,* a magazine for gifted and talented children. She enjoys ballet, modern, jazz, and tap dancing, as well as swimming, art, music, and creative writing. This multi-talented girl loves life, and "I wouldn't trade it for anything."

DAKOTA REFLECTIONS

PHOTOS BY CHERYL GORDER

PEOPLE...

Upper left: Indian Exposition at Rapid City, July 11-13, 1987.
Lower left: Bushnell Bash, September 23, 1978.
Right: Historical Festival at Fort Sisseton, June 7-8, 1986.

SEASONS.....

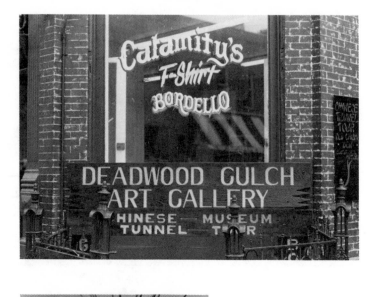

PLACES......

DAKOTA'S NATURAL WONDERS

Upper: Badlands of South Dakota.
Lower: Palisades Park, Garretson, SD.

FEATHERSTONE CASSETTE ALBUMS

TRADITIONAL

FT-1001 Gordon Bird Sings Traditional/ Contemporary American Indian Songs.

FT-1002 Dakota Songs by Wahpe Kute.

FT-1003 New Town Singers–Live at Dakota Dance Clan Celebration.

FT-1004 Mandaree Singers–Live at New Town, ND.

FT-1005 Old Scout Singers–Live at White Shield, ND.

FT-1006 Wahpe Kute–Live at Dakota Dance Clan Celebration.

FT-1007 Eagle Whistles–Live at Mandaree, ND.

FT-1008 Leroy Strong and Johnny Smith–"The Buckaroos".

FT-1009 Little Earth Singers–Live in the Twin Cities.

FT-1010 Ft. Yates Singers–Live at Ft. Yates, ND.

FT-1011 Rock Creek Singers–Live at Ft. Yates ND.

FT-1012 Mandaree Singers–Live at Bismarck ND.

FT-1013 Eagle Whistles–Live at Bismarck ND.

FT-1014 Assiniboine Singers–Live at Dakota Tipi.

FT-1-15 Dakota Tipi–Live–The Minnesota Buckaroos, Red Nation Singers, and the Assiniboine Singers.

FT-1016 Red Nation Singers–Live at Fort Totten Days.

CONTEMPORARY

FR-2001 Forty Days–Gordon Bird and the Featherstone Band.

CULTURAL-HISTORICAL

FC-3001 Dakota Language by Agnes Ross.

FC-3002 White Buffalo Calf Woman as told by Martin High Bear.

FC-3003 The Story of Iktomi as told by Vince E. Pratt.

SPECIAL PRESENTATION

FS-4001 Lakota Wiikijo Olowan by Kevin Locke.

FS-4002 All Nation Singers–Flandreau Indian School.

FS-4003 Songs of the People by Georgia-Wettlin Larsen.

FS-4004 Lakota Wiikijo Olowan by Kevin Locke, Volume 2.

FS-4005 Drummers, Dancers & Singers by R. A. Swanson.

Order from Blue Bird Publishing, 1713 East Broadway #306, Tempe AZ 85282.

OTHER BOOKS BY BLUE BIRD PUBLISHING

WHO'S WHO IN ANTIQUES
by Cheryl Gorder

The only national comprehensive directory of the antique profession! It includes auction companies, show promoters, independent antique dealers, antique mall dealers, periodicals, appraisers, services, authors, publishers, and organizations. Well-organized reference.

ISBN 0-933025-02-5 $14.95

HOME EDUCATION RESOURCE GUIDE
by Don Hubbs

Hundreds of important addresses for home schooling materials and resources. Comprehensive up-to-date lists of correspondence schools curriculums, testing services, educational toys and games, & special handicapped help.

ISBN 0-9915578-1-8 $9.00

HOME SCHOOLS: AN ALTERNATIVE
by Cheryl Gorder

Explores the controversies of home schooling and offers guidelines for parents interested in the alternative. Lists resources and home school organizations. Numerous reviews have applauded the book, including nationally recognized *Booklist* and *Small Press Book Review*. Updated 1987.

ISBN 0-933025-10-6 $11.95

Order from Blue Bird Publishing, 1713 East Broadway #306, Tempe AZ 85282.

T-Shirts

Real Dakota!

These T-shirts are made of quality 50% cotton and 50% polyester for long--lasting wear. Color: Light blue. Please state size and add shipping charges ($1.50 for first T-shirt, 50 cents each additional T-shirt.) Sizes: Adults: Extra-large, Large, Medium, Small $7.50 Childs: Large, Medium, Small $5.00

Order from:
Blue Bird Publishing
1713 East Broadway #306
Tempe AZ 85282

Checks or credit cards accepted.

Please charge my ___VISA___MC
Card#_____
Expiration Date:_____
Signature:_____
Phone #:_____

MasterCard   VISA